P9-CTA-376
HURON COUNTY LIBRARY
2 008 090956 5

SHOPKEEPERS

TO A

NATION

Mary-Etta Macpherson

SHOPKEEPERS TO A NATION

The Eatons

McCLELLAND AND STEWART
LIMITED
TORONTO MONTREAL

DESIGN: F. NEWFELD

THE CANADIAN PUBLISHERS
McClelland and Stewart Limited
25 Hollinger Road, Toronto 16

PRINTED AND BOUND IN CANADA
BY MCCORQUODALE & BLADES
(PRINTERS) LTD.

CONTENTS

PART ONE

The Founder and His Era

PART ONE

The beginning is simple enough, yet substantial too in its quiet rural way. The setting is County Antrim, Ireland's northeast corner that takes the sea's tides and weather on two sides and, behind the headlands, rolls with low mountains and river glens. Antrim's soil, of only moderate fertility, offers the farmer no easy living but a continuing challenge. A century or more ago a man who could pay regular rent on forty acres (twice the size of the average holding) and support his family in a two-storey house (twice the height of the neighbours' places) was obviously industrious and thrifty – modelled on the prototype of the hardy Ulsterman.

Such was John Eaton of the townland of Clogher, two miles north of the busy market town of Ballymena.

THE FOUNDER AND HIS ERA

For several generations the Eatons had been tenants on the Clogher farm, probably ever since their Lowland Scots ancestors had been moved by royal decree during the first "plantation" of Northern Ireland with Protestant settlers in the early 1600's. It was a pretty property: the house, standing on a rise, faced a sweeping panorama of river valley, hedged fields, and in the purple distance Slemish, the district's highest mountain where, according to Irish legend, the young St Patrick used to herd sheep for his heathen masters.

At the opening of the year 1834 John Eaton and his wife Margaret could look around them with considerable contentment and thanks to God. Their crops had been good, they owned cows, geese, and chickens, and now they could harness the horse to their new driving-car, an up-to-date rig with springs, for their trips to town. Of their eight children, the eldest, eighteen-year-old Robert, shared the farm work with his father; next came a bevy of daughters who were already proficient at churning and baking – they could be depended upon to take charge when the new baby arrived in March.

A happy picture, but within a few weeks it would be tragically altered with the death of John Eaton, following a severe chill. In due course the ninth child and fourth son was born: a fine baby who gave promise of inheriting his father's sturdy physique. Margaret Eaton named him Timothy, after one of her husband's favourite books of the New Testament.

Life at the hilltop farm continued much as before; the widow Eaton saw to that. She was a "true Craig," the Ballymena people said; member of one of the dominant Presbyterian families in the county, with the Craig good looks of blue-black hair, pink cheeks, and violet eyes, and possessing plenty of the spirit that had always marked her clan. She believed that waste and indolence were sins, that life must be a dedicated duty – even for young Tim, who was early given his work assignments, such as egg-gathering.

For him those were the pleasant years of growing up and going to school, but they were soon to be cut short by changed circumstances at home, as well as by the national disaster of famine. True, Antrim escaped the major impact of the potato failure which spread tragedy over most of Ireland, causing a million deaths between 1846 and 1851 and sending another million of the population – those with enough cash to escape – into the crowded holds of the "fever ships" sailing for New York, Boston, or Quebec.

The Eatons and their neighbours did not starve, but the harsh facts of wildly fluctuating prices, increased rents to meet skyrocketing taxes or Poor Rates, the periodic outbreak of disease, plus the total uncertainty of the future, could not be lightly dismissed. Besides, the family group was diminishing. Robert had departed for the Canadas in his twenty-fourth year, leaving the thirteen-year-old brother, John, as the man in charge of the farm. Eliza Jane had become the wife of a well-to-do neighbour, William Crabbe. Another sister, Mary, died unmarried.

No doubt these gaps in the circle, added to the general stringencies of the period, were seriously assessed, each in turn, by the widow Eaton, yet she determinedly pursued her plan for young Tim and, when he was thirteen, found the means to send him to the Academy in Ballymena for a final year of education, and more particularly, in his mother's words, "to improve his grammar." Here he came in contact with the town boys; when they teased him about his homespun clothes he fought with his back to the school wall until the challengers were satisfied. Otherwise it was a wasted year, and he was to carry a certain suspicion of secondary education for the rest of his days.

The family now decided that Timothy should learn

the business of storekeeping, and to this end he was apprenticed to one William Smith (husband of a distant Craig relative), a prosperous merchant in Portglenone, a town located on the east bank of the River Bann and about seven miles from Ballymena. Smith's drygoods shop occupied a narrow street frontage but joined a four-storey warehouse at the rear for such varied lines as feeds, hardware, liquor; there was also a landing-stage where Smith's three small cargo boats could tie up to unload goods brought from the port of Coleraine at the rivermouth.

For the most formative years of Timothy's life this was to be his round-the-clock environment six days out of seven. Often he slept on a cot under the counter – convenient when he had to get up at four in the morning on market days to serve out drams of whisky to the farmers stopping by; handy, too, late at night after he had fastened the shutters and another weary day was done. His work embraced any and all jobs, and his chief private satisfaction was derived from improving the procedures. After toting heavy sacks and crates up the warehouse ladders, he built a hand-operated hoist, and all Portglenone came to gawk at it. More daring by far, though, was his successful experiment with illuminating gas, which he had read about in a much-cherished edition of *Chambers' Encyclopædia.* The detailed description of the process whereby gas could be produced from coal too fine for fireplace use, and piped to any desired location to provide light greatly superior to oil lamps or candles, was studied step by step; finally, with the help of another apprentice, Timothy set up the equipment, showed the results to Smith, and was permitted to install the totally new lighting system in a portion of the building.

But such activities, though practical in results, were merely by way of diversion for an inventive, energetic lad trapped in a monotonous, toilsome existence. Occasionally he would be sent out with a wagon to deliver goods to the housewives; this was a pleasant break, as well as an opportunity to mention new stock just received at the store and jot down orders for the next delivery.

One job he loathed, and that was the sorting of rags bought in bulk from the pedlars who tramped the countryside. It was filthy work; dangerous too, in those years of the lice-carried typhus epidemics which had followed the famine. It was also exacting, as each type of cloth – linen, cotton, wool – had to be allocated to its own heap. After his first week with the rags, fingering and scrutinizing to determine fibre characteristics, he protested to his mother during his Sunday visit home that he was through; he begged to be allowed to stay on the farm. But this would mean forfeiture of her bond to Smith – a cash outlay the family could not afford – and so he consented to return.

Through these years he was to learn many things about merchandise and qualities and customers' ways but, more significantly, he learned about the type of employer he would never wish to be. The image of Smith and his inhumanity to the workers who did his bidding was burned into Tim's mind forever. He might have willingly accepted the sixteen-hour day, the rushed meals above the shop, even the business of the rags, if such conditions had been accompanied by ordinary Christian kindness. But Smith never relaxed the master-slave relationship. Often on a Sunday the boy, walking the nine miles to Clogher, would be caught up by the Smith carriage driving to church. Inevitably it whirled by without pause for greeting or the suggestion of a lift. In the lad standing there, brushing off the dust or the mud spatterings, was born an implacable hatred of class distinctions based on the power of wealth.

With the death of Margaret Craig Eaton in 1848, in her fifty-second year, the group at the farm lost the last strong root holding the family to its ancestral acres. There was no abrupt dispersal, yet the talk trended more and more to emigration. Good Antrim neighbours such as the Reids and Youngs had already gone; their reports from Canada West (Ontario) were encouraging. Robert Eaton, working as a lumberman near Bytown (Ottawa), wrote of the snug cabin he had built, with facing doorways; when the fire needed restoking he hitched his horse to a great hardwood log, drove into the room, rolled the wood onto the hearth, and continued on in a straight course out the other side.

Around the peat fire at home the remaining brothers and sisters reacted to these tales according to individual temperament. John, head of the house, felt no call to the Canadian bush; what he wanted was a better agricultural life for Ireland, with more schools and sweeping reform of the landlord system. But the others, including Timothy on his Sunday visits, never tired of the dream of a new life in a new country.

Suddenly a way was opened – one with romantic implications that no one could possibly have foreseen. Robert Reid, just nicely established in Georgetown, northwest of Toronto, found himself left a widower with an infant to raise; what more natural than that he should seek a wife among the Eatons back home? So a formal proposal was soon on its way by letter to Margaret, a girl still in her twenties, tall, active, happy-natured. The match must have been deemed highly suitable by the Clogher group – both the mother and first wife of the bridegroom-elect had been Craigs. Margaret made ready her trousseau, packed a trunk, said her goodbyes in 1851, and travelled several thousands of miles to her wedding in Georgetown. Robert's elegant new carriage with brass lamps carried the couple off on a touring honeymoon during which they covered almost two hundred miles of primitive roads in southern Ontario before returning, safely, to the neat brick farmhouse on the edge of town.

Now the Reids' place became the hospitable rendezvous for Eatons far and near. Nancy and Sarah came out from Ireland to stay with their sister. Robert, finished with Bytown, was a frequent visitor before moving to London and marrying one of the Antrim Youngs who had settled there. James Eaton arrived in

Georgetown and for a season or so helped with the farm work, then travelled on to join Robert.

And, finally, appeared Timothy. The year was 1854, and he had been quit of Smith's overlordship for almost two years. (But here occurs a blank in the record. Whether T. Eaton spent those two years in Ireland or, as some stories have it, emigrated immediately to Canada and worked for a time in the Maritimes and later in the Ottawa district, has never been definitely confirmed. The family belief is that he occupied himself in Antrim for most of the interval and, after disembarking at Quebec or Montreal, made a leisurely side trip to Bytown before proceeding to Georgetown. Robert's descriptions of frontier life had always fascinated the lad; undoubtedly he would want to savour it for himself.)

Margaret Reid found her baby brother grown to a broad-shouldered young man, not tall but powerfully built, ambitious, eager to learn this new country's ways, cheerful, and always ready to amuse the Reid children with comic songs. The memory of Portglenone could now be firmly locked away (though never obliterated) as an unhappy but necessary part of his training. Smith had adhered to the original apprenticeship agreement and paid his graduate one hundred pounds for the years of service, and Tim still had a little cash in his pocket after outfitting himself and buying his transatlantic passage. He could face the future in Canada with reasonable confidence.

His first job was as part bookkeeper, part clerk, in a

store at Glen Williams, a village not far from Georgetown. A year or so later he joined forces with James, who had just received the appointment of postmaster for the newly opened settlement at Kirkton in the London area. Here the brothers built a log hut for their headquarters; sister Sarah arrived to keep house, and Timothy took charge of trade with the settlers. It was raw pioneer atmosphere with few of the amenities of Georgetown, and the "T. Eaton" business lagged disappointingly; nevertheless, the Kirkton period would always be treasured by Timothy as a great turning-point in his life.

A Methodist revival campaign was underway, and after attending several meetings Timothy made the solemnly joyful discovery that this was the religion he had been seeking: a faith based on free-will acceptance of salvation, rather than on the stern Calvinist doctrine of predestination in which he had been reared. His conversion was a deeply moving experience – one he sought to share with the boys in his Sabbath School class, one he would relive many times over in future years as he watched confessed sinners and backsliders "come to the front" on the invitation of the great Methodist preachers of the day.

By 1860 James and Timothy had moved to the larger nearby community of St Marys, setting up a general store in one of the town's buff stone fronts on the main street. The earliest Eaton advertisement in existence (from St Marys *Argus,* 1861) "begs to call the attention" of old customers in the townships to the new stock of drygoods, groceries, boots and shoes, hardware, patent medicines. Brother Robert became a third partner, but later by mutual agreement he took over the teas and groceries in a separate building, while the others concentrated on drygoods under the name of "J. & T. Eaton."

It was in St Marys that Timothy met the handsome Margaret Beattie of Woodstock. She was visiting friends in town, and his eyes fell on her first at Sunday service as she walked down the aisle "like a queen," as he recalled so often in after years. Within a fortnight he contrived an introduction when they were guests at a picnic; the next year, 1862, they were married, the bride in her twenty-first year, Timothy in his twenty-eighth.

From every angle the alliance was ideal. Although born in Toronto, Margaret Beattie Eaton was thoroughly Irish in background and character. Quick-witted, volatile, outspoken whether enthusiastically for or angrily against any project, yet always having a delight in fun and mischief, she was to become the light, bright foil for Timothy's serious nature. She had an interpretive gift for poetry and drama, plus a capacity for memorizing, which might have taken her on the stage had she been born into a less strait-laced Methodist society. She rode superbly and shared her husband's love of fine horses. More, she had a practical knowledge of storekeeping from her father, who owned a successful establishment in Woodstock.

Right from the start, home and business were closely tied together for the young couple. Margaret suggested to her husband that he open a millinery department. "But," she cautioned, "the hats must be smart." He replied, "Very well, if I buy them will you trim them?" She agreed, and for the next few years, assisted by sister-in-law Sarah, she spent her spare hours surrounded with flowers, feathers, ribbon.

Though the store did sufficiently well to warrant extensions from time to time, the young merchant was far from his ultimate dream. There were frustrating conditions in any small-town enterprise serving a rural area. The scarcity of cash among the farmers meant that bartering and endless dickering were still the basis of trade. A fresh-killed lamb might be offered as payment for shoes or a bolt of gingham, but the store was left with the problem of selling the carcass, and the chances were, in a good lambing season, that this was merely the last of half a dozen accepted in such transactions – by which time the local butchers and the townspeople alike were more interested in veal or fowl. When the customer had neither produce nor money to offer, say, for the blankets and yards of flannelette needed for a new baby, a credit account was the only solution – and a year hence it might still be waiting to record its first cash payment. Under such circumstances a store's prices inevitably moved up or down according to the history of the individual purchasers and what they could pay or offer in exchange or how skilful they proved to be at the "beating-down" process.

This had always been the accepted practice in nineteenth-century storekeeping, but Timothy was not the type to embrace a fallacy, no matter how popular. He longed to try out his theory that both seller and buyer would benefit if goods were offered, and clearly ticketed, at one low cash price for all. The best place to test it, obviously, was among a wage-earning public where money circulated.

"Where shall we go, Maggie?" he asked his wife.

And she answered in her characteristic, mind-made-up way, "To Toronto."

His vote made the decision unanimous.

Early in 1869 they moved to the city, renting a house on Gloucester Street, just a few doors from Yonge. It was rather far uptown, more than a mile from the business section, but there was a stable at the back for their pony, and the yard made a good run for a few chickens, bought to provide fresh eggs for the three children: the first-born Edward Young (E. Y.), followed by Josephine and two-year-old Margaret.

Toronto was just nicely ready for its fateful encounter with the man who would carry its fame and his own around the world. From the original little colonial outpost huddled on the flats beside the bay, the town had been forced to stretch out to accommodate a population of almost fifty thousand. It had grown westward as far as the Lunatic Asylum grounds (a favourite promenade on summer Sundays), eastward to the Don River, and on the north almost to the village of Yorkville. There was hustle and bustle around the port, but the most prophetic sound of all was the long-drawn-out moan of the trains. With the new railway services, Toronto's future as the centre of trade and social life as well as the seat of the provincial government was assured. And every day new settlers with their immigrant bundles appeared on the streets.

Both place and timing seemed ideal for Timothy's great experiment, but what type of business would he launch? While he pondered that question he joined a wholesaler friend's establishment, but this was merely to mark time. Retailing on a new, better, fairer basis was his goal.

At first he gave serious consideration to the possibility of a grocery store, but there might be a grave moral impediment here – as indicated in a letter requesting advice from a Montreal expert in that field. Was it possible, Timothy asked, to do a profitable grocery trade "without licquors? . . . I have determined if Licquors is a necessary Apendix to have nothing to do with, good or bad."

Perhaps the reply discouraged the idea; at any rate it was a drygoods and haberdashery emporium that presented the Eaton name to Toronto.

The Britannia House, a small store and stock in a squat three-storey building with a 24-foot frontage on Yonge Street at the southwest corner of Queen, was purchased for a price of $6,500. It was a cash deal, made possible by the money Timothy had received from his share of the dissolved partnership in St Marys, plus a loan which he quickly arranged from a drygoods wholesaler with whom he had enjoyed friendly business relations.

With a staff of two clerks and a boy, he opened for business on December 8, 1869 – a day that was so cold Toronto Bay froze solid from shore to shore.

Timothy's project was at best a gamble, even as to location. Toronto had always shopped on fashionable King Street, some blocks south. And when the first advertisements appeared, announcing the policy of selling only for cash, and at one low price to all, the public had a good laugh. A little later when he advertised "goods satisfactory or money refunded," the local businessmen agreed that this fellow Eaton must indeed be crazy. No storekeeper had ever been known to back up merchandise with a promise of that kind; if customers got rooked, it was just their bad luck and they had no recourse.

At first, the novelty of the Eaton methods may have been a drawing-card; perhaps, too, the special "door dressing," often of large baskets heaped with special bargains – thread at 1¢ a spool, neckties at 5¢ each. But soon the immutability of the hand-printed price tickets on every item offered, and the fairness of the whole transaction captured a steady stream of trade. Customers learned they could depend on T. Eaton's word, whether in advertising or in person. On one occasion, overhearing a clerk agree with a customer's comment that "this material looks like pure wool," the proprietor spoke up firmly, "No, Madam, it is half cotton." That merchandise must be exactly as represented, and that it must be represented exactly as it was – this was a principle all Eaton employees had to learn, even in front of customers.

Much thought went into the displays and decoration, generally with the specific prodding of the merchant's wife. When "mantles" (coats and wraps) and millinery were added as a new department, one of the saleswomen appealed privately to Mrs Eaton to persuade her husband to supply hand mirrors. "He can't understand that a lady wants to see if the back of her hat is becoming." Next morning two mirrors were issued.

When a member of the staff was away ill, Margaret Eaton would set out in her pony cart to call and leave a few flowers or some home-made delicacies. Years afterwards, Eaton old-timers declared Mrs Timothy was actually "the Store's first Welfare Department."

All through this early period Timothy and James maintained a lively correspondence. They exchanged weekly sales totals – and sometimes the St Marys store was ahead by as much as forty dollars. Differences in the weather might account for a poor Toronto showing, as in the spring of 1872 when Timothy wrote to James: "my sales not so good . . . . Our ladies wont come out while it rains." The brothers' letters switched easily from business to reports of the previous Sunday's sermons, and gave the news of relatives, family births, and occasionally sorrows.

Timothy's first Toronto-born children were to die in infancy, one a daughter and the next his namesake.

In the early 1870's there was a sad, mixed-up, undated letter to James: "I have had an anxious & busy week quite different from last. We have had a birth on Tuesday. . . . A suit at the County Court on a promisory note – the jury gave us a unanimous Verdict. . . . After getting home at night our little Timothy W. fell asleep in Jesus – after 3 days suffering with Cold Brokitis took him off. . . . We are endeavoring to Trust in God. Ma & Baby is well." The new infant continued to thrive; he was named William Fletcher Eaton.

Two more children were born in the next few years, but as the youngest did not survive infancy, it was John Craig Eaton who became the smiling baby of the household. By this time Mrs Eaton had maids to help her, and the old pony cart stood next a fine carriage in the coach house behind their new residence on Orde Street, just to the south of Queen's Park and the Parliament Buildings.

From time to time Margaret Eaton accompanied her husband on his buying trips abroad, and one of their personal goals on such travels was brother John's farm at Killyree in Antrim. When the Canadian relatives arrived, "all work stopped." The wonderful presents were unpacked and exclaimed over; on one occasion John's daughters delightedly accepted a lady's bicycle, the first to be seen in that neighbourhood. There were interesting new sights awaiting the visitors' inspection as well, for John Eaton applied a progressive spirit to farming and community life much as his young brother had pursued enlightened ways in storekeeping.

A water wheel was installed to produce power for the property's flax-processing plant, and over the years several new cottages were erected for the farm hands. Most ambitious of all John's projects was the small schoolhouse, built, equipped, and staffed at his own expense for the use of the employees' and neighbours' children, along with his own large family. This was his practical method of proving the need to the local educational authorities, who eventually were graciously pleased to take over the establishment.

While Timothy made his rounds of the farm, Aunt Maggie became the vivacious centre of the group in the parlour. For months afterwards the little nieces at Killyree would practise her graceful way of walking, discuss her beautiful clothes and her thick brown hair which she let them brush at bedtime. Uncle Timothy, because he inclined to be brusque and was always asking questions, never reached the same popularity as his wife. On the other hand, Uncle James, who made an occasional visit back home, was remembered as a "playful man."

The decade of the 1880's was one of significant expansion for the Eaton business in Toronto. First came the important change of location – to the site where Eaton's of Canada still has its headquarters. The little shop at Queen and Yonge Streets had previously been able to thrust out wings as required, but by 1882 no further footage was available for purchase. In urgent need for more department space, Timothy bought three large adjoining stores in the block above Queen Street, just a little north of the old corner where his great experiment had begun. (And where the up-and-coming young Scots merchant, Robert Simpson, would soon hang out *his* sign, after a few years' tryout in a small place north of Queen. It was a sort of musical-chairs rearrangement of location for both.)

With all possible speed and enthusiasm the three shop fronts at 190-196 Yonge Street were torn down and rebuilt into a handsome new façade with long glass windows and a central entrance; the basements and three floors above ground were completely remodelled and equipped, and T. Eaton & Co. became an establishment doubled in size and requiring a staff of over a hundred. So far, so good – but there were difficulties ahead; indeed, 1883 was to be remembered by Timothy as the year when his financial resources were strained to the limit and, graver still, his onward course seemed to halt. To fill the yawning shelves, he had quickly assembled goods from local wholesalers, and it was soon apparent that the quality was not up to his usual standards. While he was anxiously assessing this situation and the lagging sales on each day's tally, a serious new problem suddenly arose. A Glasgow firm, with which he had always had amicable relations and unlimited credit arrangements, presented a sight draft for four thousand pounds for goods which he had already reported badly damaged in transit to Canada. Timothy refused to pay, but his shrewd mind saw a way to cope with all his worries at one stroke. He took the first ship to Glasgow, confronted the supplier with the facts of his case, plus samples of the water-stained merchandise, and got a proper adjustment of the account. He then went to London, told the whole story to a well-known banking house and got the necessary financial backing for an immediate Glasgow settlement. He made a lightning tour of leading British factories and exporters and ordered a shipload of the best goods – the kind, as he liked to say, "worthy of my public." When he returned to Toronto he slashed prices on all the old stock, and watched the aisles fill with bargain hunters.

A few weeks later a representative of the Glasgow firm appeared at the store to smooth matters over and explain, a little belatedly, that the former Eaton credit status had not been understood by his company's new management, and that it was hoped the good relationship of the past could continue, etc., etc. Timothy listened politely – in fact took the visitor on a carriage drive around Toronto – but the store at 190-196 Yonge Street was never again to trouble the Glasgow outfit with any orders on any basis. The famous Eaton memory, whether for kindnesses received or sharp practices attempted, had already established itself as one of the most valuable assets of the company.

Within six months the business was going forward again. It was a royal progress and all T. Eaton's decisions turned to gold. Even when he adopted a policy that seemed directly contrary to his interests, the profits continued to roll in and up.

Timothy was constantly concerned with the welfare

of his employees (whom he preferred to call "fellow associates"), and probably no businessman's campaign in local history ever surpassed in intensity his crusade for Early Closing. Before 1881 he had inaugurated six o'clock weekday closing, though all other stores stayed open till seven; with special morning bargain sales, plus a system of bonuses and percentages to his clerks, he had proved that more money could be made in a shorter workday. But for the big all-out effort to change the Toronto tradition of Saturday night shopping, when clerks had to remain on their feet till ten o'clock, it was necessary to utilize every piece of heavy artillery available.

Timothy spoke to his pastor at Elm Street Methodist Church, and soon there were resounding humanitarian appeals for Early Closing from that pulpit and others. He sought out a representative group of retailers and asked their co-operation in the movement; almost all promised, but few carried through. In the meantime, he had started his own determined campaign. In Eaton advertisements during June 1886 he challenged the women of Toronto: "Can you do all your shopping before 6 p.m. on Saturdays? Ladies, take up the agitation. . . . Liberate your fellow-beings!" He installed ballot boxes in the store and urged his customers to vote in favour of Early Closing. A few days later – perhaps the weather had turned warm – he announced new ballots for "2 p.m. closing on Saturday," an astounding innovation! And, in spite of the fact, duly reported, that 1,900 votes were for the 6:00 p.m. lockup compared with 1,500 for the Saturday half-day, Timothy blandly advertised on June 28, 1886: "Our store will close at 2 p.m. on Saturday during July and August." It was a big event in Toronto's working life, and Mr and Mrs Timothy Eaton marked the first half-holiday with a mammoth picnic in High Park for employees and their families.

The great merchant was too wise to initiate all his revolutions at once. Until 1891 his Saturday closing hour at all seasons except summer stayed at the customary 10:00 p.m. Four years later, by the time Toronto had got used to doing its Eaton shopping before six o'clock, he was ready to abandon the old policy of late store nights, even in the weeks before Christmas and Easter. At the president's year-end banquet to employees he could report that the Christmas trade during the first experiment with continuous six o'clock closing had been "very much larger" than any previous year's. His crusade had won through to a spectacular triumph, and the competition, in whatever mood of envy or reluctance, could only follow his lead.

The Eaton store was one of the first customers for electric generators designed and built in Toronto. "To the strains of music by Faust [*sic*], Wagner and Verdi, carbon arc lamps flickered throughout Eaton's for the first time on the eve of Sept. 19th, 1889," said a local paper. "That night Toronto citizens were invited to a Grand Promenade Concert in the Store," with the band of the Queen's Own Rifles supplying the music. There was no selling, just sightseeing by the community at large under the brilliant light produced by electricity generated on the premises.

The store's first telephone, installed in 1884 – located, it is believed, on the wall just outside the president's basement office – was found useful in emergencies; the consensus seemed to be that, in time, this gadget might even expedite service to customers. On the other hand, the new-fangled device called an "elevator" caused a good deal of skeptical talk. Its first day of operation saw crowds of Toronto goodwives gathered round to watch the rhythmic rise and descent of the shiny metal cage but, as not one among them would venture aboard, Timothy ordered smartly dressed wax figures to be set inside as a demonstration stimulant. By slow degrees over the next few weeks the public's fears were calmed, and shoppers began to appreciate this quicker, less tiring means of reaching the upper floors – and they were quite content with the ruling that their down trip must be made by way of the stairs. In the next few years two more elevators were installed . . . "to float up smoothly and noiselessly to the second and third floors, a distance of 65 feet," as an Eaton announcement reported.

But the project destined to dwarf all others in the early Eaton annals, and eventually to become a Canadian institution with a life uniquely its own, was of course the Mail Order Catalogue. It first saw the light of day in 1884: a modest 32-page booklet, distributed free to visitors at the Canadian Industrial Exhibition in Toronto. The cover reproduced a drawing of the

Yonge Street store; inside there was an opening greeting "To our patrons," inviting them to mail in orders for any merchandise mentioned in this Fall and Winter Catalogue, or in fact for any other type of goods wanted, and also describing the attractions of the store for visitors from out of town. . . . "When arriving at the Union Depot or by the boats, take the Yonge Street cars, as they all pass our store." The little pamphlet was bare of illustrations, but this lack was balanced by the very complete, conscientious detailing of merchandise as to materials, colours, styles, sizes, prices. "Ladies' Oiled Goat Button Boots" could be had for $1.50 per pair; the laced style cost $2.25. The sensible red-flannel era was still in vogue, as indicated by a section headed "Ladies' Scarlet Underwear"; a vest of this, "all pure wool, nicely finished," was priced at $1.00.

Visitors to the Fair took the booklets home with them, studied the pages in the lamplight of their farm kitchens, and soon the orders began to pour in. Within a few months a Company report noted with some surprise, "It has been necessary for one woman to devote her entire time to the filling of the orders, with the aid of a small boy to do the parcelling."

In 1885 the Catalogue was forty-eight pages thick; eventually, illustrations were added to provide further careful information of the merchandise offered. And right here began the important educational service of the Catalogue which Timothy could not have foreseen but which was to delight him for the rest of his days. New settlers, recently arrived in their thousands from

Europe, thumbed through each issue, page by page, over and over again, using it as a practical home textbook for study of the English language, matching the pictured item to the name and description alongside. School teachers in the prairie provinces found it helpful to keep a copy of Eaton's Catalogue in their classrooms; and there is somewhere in the Mail Order archives a letter from a priest in northern Manitoba asking if the President could possibly spare twelve copies of the new edition, as these were "most urgently required for the instruction of the children of the parish." At the same time an affectionate, personal feeling for Eaton's Mail Order service was solidly building up among the Catalogue customers from coast to coast. A farm woman in eastern Ontario shipped a basket of her choice plums to Mrs Timothy Eaton, as a mark of gratitude "for the wonderful shopping I have been able to do through your husband's Catalogue." When the railway was put through southwest of Saskatoon and the farmers were invited to name their local stations, one group unanimously agreed on "Eaton," to commemorate the friend they had in common. However, this was too close in sound to another place farther along the line, and an extra syllable was added to make it "Eatonia" – the name which both station and municipality have kept to this day.

Like the Mail Order, the Eaton factories grew from a small, almost accidental beginning. In the late 1880's the President on his rounds happened upon an unexpected tableau behind the scenes: the manager of the window-blind department in a concentrated struggle with a sewing-machine, trying, as he explained, to turn out much needed special sizes which were unprocurable from any supplier. "Get another machine and hire two women to do a proper job," Mr Eaton ordered. The experiment was a success; Toronto ladies could henceforth buy blinds readily for any height or width of window, in various qualities and colours. It was obvious that the same principle could be applied to many other lines often in short supply for a business constantly growing in volume. Men's shirts, women's underwear, and boys' knickerbockers were to follow; eventually there would be acres of floors humming with the production of merchandise ranging all the way from horse harness to women's furs, and for many years Eaton's advertising and Catalogue pages frequently carried the proud line across the bottom, "Made in Our Own Factories."

As the last years of the century ticked off, Timothy Eaton had become the acknowledged king of a realm, head of "Canada's greatest store," the editorial writers agreed, merchandiser to a whole nation through the Mail Order, employer of 2,500 workers who called him, sometimes with affection, always with respect, "The Governor." It was perhaps only to be expected that he would have his detractors and imitators too.

Oddly enough, one of his boldest rivals for a short period was John Weldon Eaton, a nephew. He was the son of his brother James, who in the 'eighties had sold out the St Marys business to Robert Eaton's son, had started up again in London, but finally moved to Toronto to spend his declining years. John Weldon Eaton was a dashing playboy type, follower of the horse races, and in business hours full of promotion schemes – a go-getter long before the term was invented. He opened a department store on Yonge Street, two blocks below his uncle's, stocked it with similar lines – carpets, dress goods, ready-to-wear – and in large-space advertisements proclaimed "littler prices than elsewhere. . . . Our new store is teaching older ones by example!"

All this Uncle Timothy might have swallowed without comment, but the name of the new firm, "The J. Eaton Co.," was just too impertinently close to that of "The T. Eaton Co.," and the old man, probably as much in anger as in sorrow, hauled his nephew into court and won the case. Hereafter the new store was to be known as "The John Eaton Co." But its days were numbered. In 1897 the building burned to the ground, three hundred employees were thrown out of work, and John Weldon Eaton moved to New York where he died three years later.

What sort of man was Timothy Eaton, who in twenty to thirty years could create a mercantile empire with nothing but his own work and inner convictions? A full portrait at this distance is hardly possible, yet there are illuminating glimpses still worth seeking out from past records and family memories. He believed profoundly in personal integrity in business, and his restless search for quality was directed even more toward men's minds and characters than to the merchandise they would sell. Almost all his relatives were invited at one time or another to join his organization. Many accepted, but if they failed to measure up he dismissed them as summarily as he would a lazy parcel boy. There was an awesome crisis – still somewhat of a mystery – which he resolved with the overnight firing of three trusted directors, one of them his sister Eliza Jane's grandson.

Timothy was a man of few words, and they were delivered in a crisp, quick way. He had early learned, and admitted, that this trait unsuited him for face-to-face dealings with shoppers at the counter. He had a fondness for slogans and mottoes, one of them being "the greatest good for the greatest number," which he found applicable to both customers and employees. He could quote the Bible effectively for any type of occasion. His remarks at an annual meeting of directors concluded with, "Go to the ant, thou sluggard, consider her ways and be wise"; business, he declared, would improve if each man present would take the earliest opportunity to study "what goes on at an ant hill."

For years he had written his own advertising; when pressure of expansion necessitated turning this duty over to a department, he passed on the following note in his own vigorous, sprawling handwriting (a scrap of paper reverently guarded by managers there for many years): "Tell your story to public – what you have and what you propose to sell. Promise them not only bargains but that every article will be found just what it is guaranteed to be. Whether you sell a first rate or a 3rd rate article, the customer will get what they bargain for. . . . Use no deception in the smallest degree – nothing you cannot defend before God and Man."

In all the ways essential to mercantile success Timothy Eaton was a total modern, even a revolutionist; yet he had little use for much of the paraphernalia that would soon become indispensable to twentieth-century business: memos, wordy reports, downtown clubs, head tables, personal publicity. Most of his philanthropy was done in secret, often on the spur of the moment. One day in the middle of a long, severe winter he dropped in at the store's employment office to see the manager. "There must be quite a few of our people away, sick and in need," he said. "I want you to use this to help them," he went on, handing over a cheque for three thousand dollars, drawn on his private account. "When it's all gone, let me know." Out of such informal incidents and the concern that prompted them was to grow the welfare service with its branches of nursing and medical help, sick-visiting and emergency financial aid where required.

Away from the store Timothy Eaton's chief interests were church and home. In the 1890's he ensconced his family in one of the city's grandest new residences, a rambling mansion at the northwest corner of Spadina Road and Lowther Avenue, a new district to the northwest of central Toronto. (The building is now the national headquarters of the IODE, a gift to this women's organization from an Eaton daughter, Josephine.) In its family heyday the house was much admired for its size; it was almost as big as Government House on King Street, ample with corridors, staircases, fireplaces, palm-filled conservatories, reception rooms hung with *pointe de Venise* lace curtains, and furnished with French gilt chairs and rich ornaments in countless numbers on display in glass cabinets and on every available inch of flat surface.

At home, Timothy was always "Father," and for years his name for his wife was simply "Mother."

Any guests who might happen to be staying with the Eatons over the weekend would inevitably find themselves at morning service with the family in the regular pew at nearby Trinity Methodist, the church which Timothy and a few other gentlemen, including his nephew John Crabbe, a senior executive with the Toronto *Star*, had recently founded on Bloor Street in the developing area "uptown."

A careful mother could send her daughter to the Eaton home with perfect confidence: it was one of the few great mansions where cards, dancing, and any drink stronger than tea were totally banned. But Margaret Eaton's hospitality was famous. At Sunday dinner, as butler and maid hovered about behind the guests, the hostess would call out merrily, "Eat hearty and give the house a good name." Sometimes at the end of the meal, guests would be amazed to see a small bowl of cold mashed potatoes and a jug of buttermilk placed before the host, who would proceed to pour the latter over the former and eat the mixture with great relish.

This was one of his favourite Irish combinations but, rather than interrupt his wife's meticulously planned menu, he waited till after dessert for his special dish.

Timothy loved to sit at the head of a long tableful of people, especially if they were The Family. He made it a point to remember the names of all the Eatons, even down to the latest third-generation newcomer. He was their patriarch, their tribal chieftain. Some within the connection resisted his supremacy, some turned away, and their sons and daughters were to grow up unacquainted with their Toronto cousins. But not one among them was so foolish, so blind, or so bitter as to deny that the fatherless boy from Clogher had indeed "done well."

PART TWO

Knighthood in Full Flowering

PART TWO

A new era was about to open. The nineteenth century prepared to bow out – a little dizzy no doubt after all it had accomplished. Within that span of a hundred years Canada's major industry had switched from beaverskins to wheat, her transportation from birchbark canoe to steam or electric power, and her retail trade, at least in the booming city of Toronto, from primitive barter to Eaton's Friday Bargain Day – and the chance to buy such essentials as "ladies' gray flannel drawers, all wool, heavy flossed, regular $1, for 55¢."

The store had been extended north, west and south, until it occupied almost the whole of the city block which is the centre of Eaton operations today. The Mail Order Department would have to move soon to its huge new building where its own buyers, managers, and staff would speed the funnelling in and out of orders received from some 200,000 Catalogues in circulation, and where its separate stock of merchandise, ranging all the way from hairpins to ploughs, was to be as efficiently departmentalized as the main store's. The first new all-factory building, opened in 1893, was already becoming desperate for more space, especially to house the sewing-machines required for ladies' coats and capes – a recent successful experiment that probably presaged the development of Canada's cloakmaking industry. Buying-offices had been set up in London and Paris to ensure a flow of quality merchandise – everything from books and china to dress fabrics and millinery trimmings

– for the Toronto emporium's show windows and special departments.

Things had happened fast for the Eatons of Toronto, yet the first few years of the twentieth century would see an even greater acceleration. And by one of those curious caprices of history, there would be a sudden change of face as well as pace, with significant interaction between the two.

Timothy Eaton had made it no secret that his eldest son, Edward Young Eaton, would inherit the presidency. From his seventeenth year, E. Y. had been his father's first lieutenant; both he and the organization had grown up together. When he was twenty he was put in charge of the city delivery system, smoothing out the details of parcel wrapping, addressing, fixed times for collecting and assembling at the dispatch door where the three wagons stood ready. The dark blue, red, and white colour scheme of the Eaton trucks in 1963 was E. Y.'s choice for his shining, high-wheeled turnouts (carefully washed down each evening), also for the wintertime sleighs which announced themselves merrily, street by street, with the jingling of harness bells. The big dapple-grey horses which he bought with an eye for perfect matching were to add to their numbers year by year, and one of the sights of Toronto's pre-motoring years was the double procession of Eaton wagons moving off from the dispatch doors of the store, each horse as completely disciplined as to timing and route as the uniformed driver in charge.

With the organizing of the delivery system and innovations such as the pneumatic-tube service for the handling of cash, E. Y. had made himself a sort of speed-up engineer of merchandising. He enjoyed detail, however minute. It was his habit to go through the store every morning, memo pad in hand, and check on anything that caught his eye, from untidy shelves or scuffed flooring to, it is alleged, various attractive new faces among the salesgirls.

No one can say now what might have been the course of Canada's greatest retailing business if E. Y. had been permitted to live out his business destiny – for this was not to be. Toward the end of 1900, in his thirty-seventh year, he was struck down with diabetes, the disease which in those days could have but one result. With his death the E. Y. family – consisting of two pretty daughters, whose mother had died in her twenties, and their devoted stepmother, Mabel Eckhardt Eaton – ceased to participate in store management.

The blow to Timothy Eaton and his plans was a heavy one. For the past year The Governor had been making a painful convalescence from injuries received in a driving accident; on his way home from the Eaton farm west of Toronto his high-stepping pair of horses had taken fright and bolted, throwing him to the curb and shattering his thigh. He had gradually gained sufficient strength to go to the store for a few hours each day, sitting in a wheelchair most of the time; nevertheless, it had been necessary to relax much of the firm grip he had formerly kept on the business.

Now, more than ever, it was imperative to have the right man as second in command.

Who would it be? To appreciate the answer, it is necessary to draw closer for a look at Timothy's adult family.

The two daughters had married men quite outside the mercantile sphere. Josephine's husband, T. D. M. Burnside, was a Britisher who preferred English country life to the Toronto scene. Whether it was this unadaptability, or his in-laws' lack of warmth toward him, or private disagreement between himself and his wife on the rearing of their children, is not completely clear (and all these explanations are still discussed among the relatives), but after a few years the marriage ended in separation. Mr Burnside returned to England; "Josie" was to become an inveterate traveller and connoisseur-collector of period furniture and china; their son Alan and daughter Iris shuttled back and forth between their parents at intervals.

Margaret Eaton, Timothy's second daughter, almost as handsome as her mother and with much of that lady's ebullience of temperament, had married Charles E. Burden. They had met in downtown Sunday School, and their wedding was the first to take place in Trinity Methodist Church. Charlie Burden remained with the paint manufacturing company in which he had started as a poor "Cabbagetown" boy in his early 'teens; he was to move up, rung by rung, until he headed the firm. The Burdens' two sons and two daughters grew up in a lively, well-to-do home where everyone was encouraged to have a hobby – like Mother, with her needlework and her welfare clubs, or Dad, with his gardening and Masonic activities.

William Fletcher Eaton was the happy-go-lucky maverick among Timothy's offspring. Even in appearance he was different, with red hair, jutting ears, and a perpetually quizzical, boyish expression in his eyes. After leaving school in his 'teens, he had held several jobs in the store, his first post being the traditional one at a parcelling desk. (Thirty years later he still prided himself on his proficiency with paper and boxes and string – even to the point of insisting on rewrapping his household's piles of Christmas gifts as they accumulated for delivery. "Once a parcel boy, always a parcel boy," he would cheerfully declare.)

But before the end of the century Bill had left his father's organization – and perhaps that was the most striking proof of his non-conformity. He had married the beautiful Norah Cook, niece of Eaton's chief timekeeper, Joe Cook, who is still remembered as the inaugurator of Company hockey teams in the exciting days before the "pros" dominated the ice. Bill and Norah, romantically determined to make their life together a special adventure, had joined the settlers' trek to the prairies; with no experience of farming or lonely isolation or Manitoba winters, they attempted to break a quarter-section of new land to wheat. After a couple of desperate years they sold out and returned to their hometown, and Bill became manager of a small woollen mill. Later he would be summoned back by his father to handle the new Eaton whitewear factory in Oshawa, but at this moment of decision in the autumn of 1900 Bill was as remote from store politics and operation as if he were still struggling with a rusted crop on the great plains.

There was just one obvious and logical choice for a new Vice-President, and that was the youngest of all the main-line Eatons: John Craig, just twenty-four years old. Before the twentieth century got properly underway, the official announcement of his appointment appeared. A glittering new phase for both the Eaton family hierarchy and the store had begun.

At the time of the promotion, Jack Eaton held an executive position in the main office, and he had been a director on the Company board for several years. Nevertheless the sudden elevation was a little startling.

"Father," he asked, "what do I have to do as Vice-President?"

"Can you say 'Yes' and 'No'?"

"Yes, I can do that."

"Can you decide which you want to say at the right time?"

"Well, that might be different."

"But it's all you have to do."

He was used to these pithy brevities from his father; there had been plenty of opportunity to observe how much instinctive judgement, plus careful experience, was embedded in each.

Jack's first venture into selling had been as a six-year-old at Christmastime; as a special treat he was allowed to stand beside a box of giant tops in the Toy Department, set them spinning one by one, and accept each customer's quarter with a well-drilled "Thank you." His school years at Upper Canada College – where both he and brother Bill had classes with a certain young master named Stephen Leacock – were punctuated by many Saturdays of earning spare cash at the store. Frequently he worked in the boiler room, and from those days sprang his lifelong passion for engines and oilcans.

In his late 'teens Jack became a full-time Eaton's employee, posted to Notions, then Dress Goods and other sections. In his twentieth year he was packed off by his father on a few hours' notice to accompany the store's senior buyer on a round-the-world trip that covered the leading markets of the Orient, the Mediterranean, and northern Europe. In Paris Jack saw some novelty dress fabrics at four dollars a yard; in spite of his companion's protests at the "outrageous" price, Jack insisted on placing a sizable order. "Don't worry," the young man said. "These goods will go like a stampede of forty-niners." Two months later they did.

Such successes did not surprise his father, but they were talked about by others less shrewd in character analysis. Many people viewing Jack from a distance were inclined to say he was too young, too happy, too good-looking, too popular, and too rich from the outset, to be his father's successor. And wasn't it time for him to settle down? Toronto society's brightest girls, assisted by their mothers, were eager to help with this particular project, but so far he had eluded capture. At least once there had been the rumour of a formal engagement, but the story goes that his parents, after entertaining the young lady for a weekend at their Muskoka place, applied their power of veto.

Thus he was saved for the great love of his life, and a partnership that was to radiate a beneficent influence far beyond the confines of one home or even one business realm.

It happened that Jack developed a minor ailment. The Eatons' family doctor prescribed a few days in hospital and sent him to Rotherham House, one of a number of exclusive private establishments which served Toronto's rich sick sixty years ago. The young man wasn't really ill; by the second day he was up and dressed, and probably restless with boredom behind his newspaper, when a light, feminine voice from the doorway announced a message just received for Mr Jack Eaton over the downstairs telephone. He looked up – and the tedium of time and place vanished as he greeted the hospital's newest student nurse, the girl with the pompadour of shining golden hair, pink-and-white complexion and wide-set eyes. Her name was Flora McCrea and she had celebrated her twentieth birthday just a few weeks before. Next day Nurse McCrea thought it odd that she should encounter this new patient so often – on the stairway, in the drawing-room, along the corridors – but before a week had passed she realized that what had started as a casual accident was rapidly becoming a young man's plan of campaign. A few days after his departure for home she received a dinner invitation from Mrs Timothy Eaton. Jack called for her with horse-and-buggy, knowing she preferred that to the uncertain novelty of his White Steamer automobile, and so, for the first time, and wearing her good Sunday dress, Flora McCrea was welcomed into one of Canada's wealthiest homes as the most important guest of the occasion.

It must have been an ordeal for a girl just a few months away from the familiar security of village life, but the Eatons were cordial, and indeed the more they knew of Flora and her background, the more they marvelled at their son's good luck, and theirs. Like the Eatons, the McCreas had emigrated from Northern Ireland around the time of the Black Famine; they had settled in Omemee, a little hamlet about seventy miles northeast of Toronto, and situated midway between the market town of Lindsay on the west and the much larger community of Peterborough on the east. They were staunch Methodists, and the family of eight children, of whom Flora was the youngest, had been brought up to participate regularly in the duties of church and home. They knew a good deal about storekeeping too, Uncle Isaac McNeilly being a well-established merchant on the main street, and Flora's father, John McCrea, the cabinetmaker of the district, having a small shop-front which occasionally his little girl would be sent to mind after school hours.

The courtship proceeded at whirlwind pace (Jack

was never a dawdler at any enterprise) and, with the blessings of the two sets of parents, the engagement was announced in March 1901, and the wedding followed on May 8. The whole countryside roundabout Omemee was caught up in the social furore. The weekly papers in the nearby towns sent their special observers to cover the event, and one of them was moved to report that "all the rubber-tired carriages from Lindsay and all the rubber-necked people from Omemee were at Miss Flora McCrea's wedding." The Wesleyan Methodist Church was filled with guests – those from Toronto having been conveyed in Timothy Eaton's special train – and all the whisperers reached unanimous agreement that there had never been a prettier bride, so fair, so slim in her shirred and flounced white chiffon over taffeta, nor a handsomer groom, with his rippling chestnut hair, square-cut face, and eyes and mouth beaming with the smile that included everyone. A fairy-tale romance carried to its finale – and it was understandable when some of Flora's schoolgirl friends were heard to wonder aloud, at the reception that taxed the capacity of the McCreas' modest house, if there was a Jack *Simpson* in Toronto too.

After a Muskoka honeymoon Jack and Flora settled in the completely furnished new house which had been his parents' wedding gift. It was a medium-sized three-storey building on Walmer Road, just a short walk from the Timothy Eatons' big mansion on the next street, and the providential circumstance of an adjoining vacant lot offered Jack the opportunity to build a garage.

At that time, the word itself was totally foreign to Toronto ears, yet the young man, characteristically, had such intuitive belief in the forthcoming motoring age that he ordered space for two cars, though he possessed only one. Eventually the Electric bought for his wife would share the facilities with his new Winton, which proudly bore Ontario's No. 1 licence.

Right from the start Flora found it necessary to study the strict protocol of Toronto society. Before her marriage she had never owned an evening gown; now she required a wardrobe of them, as full dress for both ladies and gentlemen was *de rigueur* at concerts, theatres, and even the smallest dinner parties. She must announce her day "at home," but she discovered there was no freedom of choice, as by some mysterious decree *all* hostesses north of Bloor Street (her district) were expected to stay in on Fridays for their callers and snowstorms of cards, whereas ladies living south of Bloor did their receiving on Thursdays.

Jack, having come from a well-staffed home, was used to being waited upon, but he readily adjusted his habits to a household equipped with one servant, and learned to organize his own areas such as clothes closet and shoe-polishing kit. Once, when a young man from England was staying overnight and in the time-honoured British way had left his shoes outside the guest-room door, Jack stealthily set to work at seven the next morning, gave them a fine polish, put them back in place and, knocking on the closed door, announced in an assumed English voice, "Bath, sir." The visitor was never to know who his good bootblack had been.

The young couple delighted in their new home, and guests for dinner or weekends were frequent. Jack, in particular, loved the impromptu occasion. One day when husband and wife had planned to go to the afternoon baseball game, he telephoned from the office and said, "I'll be coming up for you as arranged, darling, and I'm bringing guests: the Crown Prince and Princess Rupprecht of Bavaria." She gasped in dismay, but he hastened on: "They're just people, like you and me. I think you'll like them." He was right of course, and after the game the foursome returned to the house for the simple dinner of the type Jack enjoyed. Chops and rice pudding were favourite menu items.

Flora's education in Company affairs had also started early. With her husband as guide, she had toured all sections, including the delivery stables. Often she spent a morning walking beside her father-in-law's wheelchair as his attendant steered him slowly through the various store departments. A fine cameraderie had sprung up between Timothy Eaton and "Florrie McCrea," as he always called her, and years later she would declare it was the Governor himself who trained her in Eaton policies.

Two events that caused great rejoicing in the Jack Eatons' household in those early years of marriage were to occur some two summers apart. In May 1903 their first child, Timothy Craig, was born; and, as the first of Timothy's grandsons to bear his surname, the baby had a royal welcome indeed. In July 1905 the founder insisted that his namesake participate in what was to go down in Company annals as one of the historic Eaton occasions: the opening of the Winnipeg Store – which in its own way was Jack's baby too.

For some years the Vice-President had been urging a complete branch operation to serve the rapidly growing West. His father was willing to listen to the proposition, but some of the directors were skeptical; Jack, they said, had not sufficient maturity of judgement for a matter of such magnitude. Finally, after Jack turned in a detailed report following an on-the-spot investigation, Mr Timothy gave his approval for a six-storey building to cover one of Winnipeg's city blocks; the recommended property at the corner of Portage Avenue and Hargrave Street was purchased and the work of excavation begun. But at head office in Toronto a few weeks later consternation broke out afresh. E. R. Wood, the well-known financier and a close friend of Timothy Eaton, returned from a western trip and immediately called on the President to offer his considered opinion of the new venture: "There's a hole in the ground there so big that it will never be needed during your lifetime or mine!" Mr Eaton, deeply troubled, summoned his son and, as always, came to the point immediately. "John, do you think five floors will do?" Although still confident of his original scheme, Jack agreed.

The Winnipeg opening is still talked about in the family as one of the great Eaton events. The President had chartered a private car and sleeper for the train trip;

a large furnished house was taken over to accommodate all members of his party for their week in Winnipeg. At the store's opening ceremonies the gravely smiling, white-bearded founder held the two-year-old Timothy on his lap, and from his wheelchair guided the child's fingers to press the button which swung wide all the doors simultaneously. Thousands of people rushed in on an inspection tour of their city's first modern department store. Later there were speeches of felicitations from representatives of church, state, and business. And when the selling began, each lady of the family took up her assigned position on the main floor: Mrs Jack Eaton in the Ribbon Circle, Mrs Burden in the Ladies' Handkerchiefs, and Mrs E. Y. Eaton at a cash register, while the President's wife moved about as a dignified supervisor. For one hour's work they were paid fifty cents apiece, issued in cheque form. The men of the group expressed some envy; they had had no chance to "earn money," as they hurried about, examining all the details of equipment and operation, and meeting the staff. A nucleus of experienced personnel had been sent out earlier from the Toronto store to set up the new departments and services and train new employees; it is an interesting footnote in Eaton history that almost all persons among that eastern contingent elected to stay on and become enthusiastic Westerners.

The success of Jack's brain-child was to secure him a permanent place among twentieth-century mercantile geniuses. Within a few months the Eaton employees in Winnipeg had to be increased from the initial 700 to

1,000; before two years had passed the missing sixth floor had been rushed to completion for much-needed expansion. The Winnipeg Store (always capitalized in this manner in Company records) was prophetic of the far-off future when The T. Eaton Co., Ltd. would become "Eaton's of Canada" with a business empire stretching from coast to coast.

Timothy Eaton was not to see the full maturing of this western project. Quite unexpectedly, after two or three days' illness at home with a chest cold and fever, he passed away, at the age of seventy-three, on Thursday morning, January 31, 1907. Within hardly more than an hour, all Eaton stores, factories, and foreign buying offices had lowered their blinds and ceased operations until the following Monday. At the funeral, held in the Eaton residence, one of his pastors and great friends declared to the hushed throng of mourners that "Timothy Eaton's success was as great in his own line as that of the Fathers of Confederation," and predicted that the influence of his fair-dealing and concern for his fellow man would be felt by generations yet unborn. The long route to Mount Pleasant Cemetery was lined with citizens to whom his name had for years been as familiar as their own.

Only three of Timothy Eaton's immediate connection of contemporaries survived him. His spinster sister, Sarah, was still alive, spending her last years with her Reid nieces and nephews in Georgetown, and occupying her time with the fine knitting for which there was a constant demand in Eaton's Baby Wear Department. Sister Nancy, who had long ago married George Young, a widower with five children, had reached final invalidism in her small neat house in St Marys; she, too, had plenty of memories of storekeeping hazards and triumphs, as her one child, William G., had become a prosperous jeweller in London, and two stepsons, Milton J. and Robert J., owned shops in Brantford and London respectively.

And there was, of course, the wife who had been Timothy's unfailing support through almost a half-century of crowded hours. Just a few weeks before his last illness, the President had said to his son, "Always take good care of Mother, Jack – Mother's grand!"

"Mother" was to live on into her nineties, a handsome and regal figure to the end, cherished by all her family, and season by season, busy with hospitable occasions at the three residences: the Toronto mansion, the small country estate in nearby Oakville, and her beloved *Ravenscrag* on Muskoka's Lake Rosseau. Everywhere her rooms became more and more filled with mementoes of family and friends, for she was an ardent accumulator in the approved tradition of a nineteenth-century chatelaine. She continued with her outside interests as well, notably the finishing school, unique in Canada, which her husband had founded and built in her name: The Margaret Eaton School of Literature and Expression – a graceful structure in the classic Greek style, containing stage and auditorium and classrooms, where young ladies could learn the

Glimpses of a Century's Growth

The first "T. Eaton & Co." emporium
as it looked on opening day when
Toronto shoppers were invited
to examine the big stock
of dry goods and
haberdashery

ASHLEY DRUGS
DRUGS
ANIMAL HEALTH
BEAUTY AIDS
DRUGS

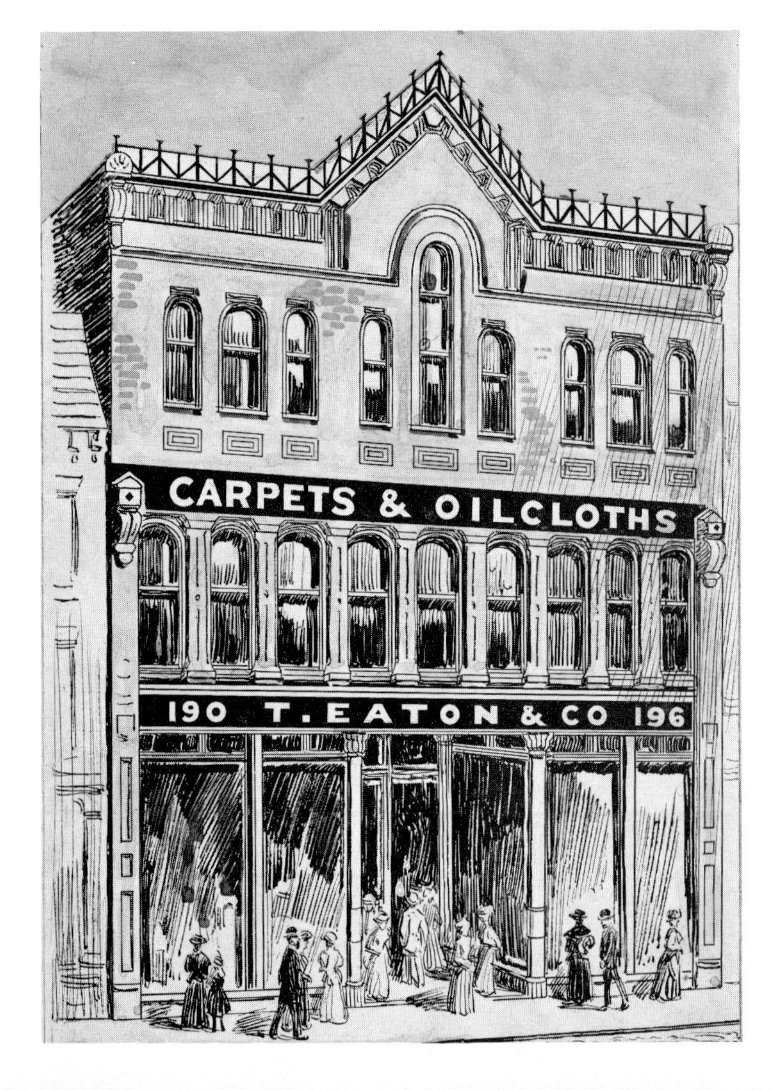
CARPETS & OILCLOTHS
190 T. EATON & CO 196

1860-9: Before coming to Toronto, Timothy was partner with his brother in dry-goods business in this St Marys store

1883 was the year of expansion into this impressive building, replacing three shop fronts on Yonge Street, north of Queen

1913: One of the first escalators in the Toronto store

One of the sights of Toronto in the pre-motorized age: Eaton's dark blue, red, and white delivery wagons and well-groomed horses waiting to depart, two abreast, from the James Street side of the main store cluster

Eaton's–College Street, the store that has sometimes been described as "the crown jewel" in the Company chain. Main section is given over chiefly to house furnishings; auditorium and restaurant on top floor

EATON'S OF CANADA
EATON'S

Luncheon buffet, plus a magnificent view, in Eaton's Marine Room restaurant atop the main store in Vancouver

Today's trend in Eaton store architecture: the Halifax Shopping Centre, with plenty of adjacent parking space

Eaton's takes its service to the suburbs: the gala opening at Don Mills Shopping Centre, Toronto

Looking toward the main entrance of Eaton's Service Centre near Toronto. The building is just a few feet less than one mile in circumference, has internal roadway system, plus safety rules, for stock transportation.

principles of poise, voice control, diction, and interpretation of drama and verse.

A few years after her husband's death, Mrs Eaton launched forth on a special memorial project which she knew would fulfil one of his dreams: the building of a church that would welcome people of all faiths, would be open every day to offer solace, moral strength, and inspiration to all age groups. Jack immediately joined her in the undertaking, and in 1914 the plan became a reality with the dedication of Timothy Eaton Memorial Church, a great grey-stone building, beautifully designed and detailed, and occupying a wide sweep of some of Toronto's most expensive property in the heart of a fine residential section. From its first Sunday of services the church became one of the busiest in the city; churchmen from afar made a point of visiting it and studying the facilities and activities. Most of the family members have worshipped there over the years, and many well-known figures among the store's officers and employees; it was probably inevitable that local wits would revise the name, as they did, to "St Timothy and All Eatons."

People who had predicted sweeping changes in Company operation under John Craig Eaton suffered a bad case of discomfiture as they observed the new President at work. Timothy Eaton's policies continued, even down to the little matters that have added so much piquancy to store folklore. The Governor had disapproved of smoking; thus there have never been cigarette or tobacco counters in any Eaton store to this day. The Sabbath was made for rest and worship; hence all store windows and their merchandise displays must be curtained from public view on Sundays. And because in Timothy's day, afternoon Sabbath School, ending at four o'clock, was an important part of the weekend program, it is still not permissible for any Eaton staffer to start a Company business trip on Sunday before the stroke of four o'clock.

All such traditions were scrupulously honoured by "Mr J. C." The Company had always been under the control of one head – and that was the way it would continue. There were no sudden churnings of Board or top management. Timothy Eaton's executive group carried on: his wife, as Honorary President, and his daughter, Mrs Burnside, as active member of the Board of Directors, which also included a few of the firm's senior men who had been permitted to buy shares after the incorporation of the Company in the 1890's. Officers and department heads stayed put, and among these were several of Jack's cousins: two sons of Uncle Robert Eaton – John James, manager of an Eaton factory, and Robert Wellington, the popular Toronto store superintendent for many years; and, importantly for the future, the last of the County Antrim Eatons to move to Canada – Robert Young Eaton, "R. Y.," who had risen to Company secretary.

A year or so before Timothy died he was asked by a downtown acquaintance how much larger he expected the Eaton enterprise would eventually become. "I cannot say," the President replied. "All I know is that I have been too low in each of my previous estimates. The long future will depend on the men who come after me."

With Mr J. C. in command, the great organization pushed ahead in many spheres. The Toronto store was enlarged, the Mail Order expanded, and the Catalogue would henceforth be printed on Eaton's own presses; between 1907 and 1913 buying-offices were opened in New York, Manchester, Belfast, Berlin, and Leicester. In 1912 a new ten-storey building joined the Eaton complex around Toronto's City Hall. Here, furniture and home equipment and even completely decorated "houses" would be presented to the public. One large area set apart as an automobile display room, where such models as the Chalmers and the Waverley Electric ("a good Easter gift for wife or daughter") stood in gleaming array, was closed down after the first year; motorcars were just too costly to be purchased on Eaton's all-cash basis.

The Shopping Service grew swiftly and logically out of a friendly little column headed, "You Were Inquiring?" which appeared at intervals in the daily-paper advertising of 1911, and which answered such anxious questions from readers as "Is it correct to leave the white cloth on the table between meals, or should you always replace it by a coloured cloth?" From such a beginning it was an easy step for the correspondent to order the recommended coloured cover or new-style ecru lace scarf, and to know that, while unable to come to the store herself, she would benefit by the good judgement of a Shopping Service expert.

"Special Attractions" began to multiply. The Governor had long ago recognized a big store's place in community life and interests. He had hung out his banners on the city's fiftieth anniversary, and in 1893 Peary's first attempt to reach the North Pole was staged in realistic miniature. "Bring the children," invited the newspaper announcements, and thousands of young and old crowded in to look with awe at the scene: hummocky expanses of snow and ice, the gallant little ship caught fast, the lonely, moving figures of the explorer and his comrades, and over all the play of northern lights from the dark dome of the long Arctic night.

Now, with Mr J. C.'s leadership, such occasions extended in number and scope. In 1913 Eaton's brought the world-famous Paris fashion designer, Paul Poiret, to Toronto, staged three lectures and demonstrations by him in the largest local theatre – and, even at that, disappointed hundreds of women who had been a little slow in picking up the free cards of admittance. From this beginning came the twice-yearly fashion shows with parades of live models and bridal entourages, accompanied by orchestral music and sometimes afternoon tea. Leading interior decorators such as Professor Frank Alvah Parsons of New York gave special lecture series on house furnishings in all its phases. The game of golf, just starting to capture local attention, was explained and demonstrated by experts for downtown businessmen at the noon hour. It was expected that their wives, of course, would be more interested in the classes for knitting, needlework, and fruit-preserving which had their turns at specified seasons.

No special attraction, however, could compare in total community appeal with the Santa Claus Parade – believed to be the first in commercial history anywhere in the world. Again, this grew from a modest start. In 1903 the manager of the Toys installed a beaming live Santa to greet the pre-Christmas crowds of children. Two years later the jolly old fellow made a public arrival at the store in a wagon swathed in bunting, and Toronto, watching from the curb, loved it. From that point forward Santa's annual appearance on the main streets in November was to become a big, joyous, fixed event in Toronto's calendar, as inevitable as Christmas Day itself.

No one took more uninhibited pleasure in the parade than Jack Eaton, and characteristically he enjoyed adding his own touches. In 1911 he had Santa start his trip actually from the north, namely the town of Newmarket: the procession of tally-hos, band, and costumed marchers was cheered on its way by the farmers' families, then halted overnight at a hotel on the city outskirts; next morning the President joined it and rode down Yonge Street at its head. In 1919 he decreed a thoroughly modern opening with the arrival of the old gentleman by air; milling thousands around the flying-field shouted themselves hoarse as the scarlet-clad figure stepped from the open cockpit of the little plane and took his place in the parade formation. But perhaps the most popular event of Jack's years was the time when live reindeer pulled Santa along on his sleigh float. The commotion of planning, involving Toronto, Ottawa, and the Grenfell Mission in Labrador, has left echoes in Eaton records to this day. Nevertheless, four small dainty reindeer arrived in the early autumn in a keeper's charge; they had been terrified of the noise of their freight ride between Quebec City and Toronto, and nervously skittish on the trip from station to the President's private stables, but week by week, with care and training, they came to accept the new environment. On the great day they behaved perfectly, even in the roaring din of the thousands lining the streets. They were to spend the rest of their lives on a Company executive's farm, surrounded by peace and quiet and good foraging, with nothing to disturb them except some wildly improbable memories.

The President made it a point to ride in the parade year by year – at least once, it is rumoured, in costume. He never lost his delight in the event or in the public for whom it was so carefully designed. When the youngsters spontaneously addressed letters to Santa Claus, c/o Eaton's, a special answering service was speedily set up, and every child's message was acknowledged by a personal reply on Santa's own stationery. From time to time Mr J. C. enjoyed looking over the incoming mail and finding such helpful information as "Dear Santa: I am ten years old. In case you bring me some thing too small for me. So I would like you to no my age. . . ."

In all these activities having to do with the great mercantile organization, John Craig Eaton was typically his father's son; in other ways he was entirely his own man. He loved to be among people. He liked the joviality of an all-men's gathering, and he could be a contributor as well as a listener, for he was never without a fund of dialect stories. Among women he became the gay gallant, with an inborn gift for making a few pleasantries convey a memorable compliment. He had, in short, charm – of the effortless, unselfconscious kind.

He enjoyed the good things of life, and among them he counted his whisky and his monogrammed cigars – but on Company premises he was scrupulous about obeying the strict rule for all employees: total abstinence from both. Occasionally he would move a Board meeting from the store to his house where everyone could relax with a smoke and a drink. Men who worked with him maintain that he never permitted himself to be angered by business problems; he trusted his advisers to bring all the angles to his attention, and then he would move buoyantly, confidently ahead to the most practical solution.

His love affair with the internal combustion engine never lost its first fine rapture. When his model K Packard was delivered, Jack posed at the wheel for the newspaper photographers, and under the heading, "Finest Automobile in Canada," the caption highlighted the amazing details: "speed from three to 55 miles an hour . . . seven people can be accommodated . . . engine has enough power to run up a steep incline at the rate of

25 miles an hour . . . canopy and side curtains . . . and the car costs as much as a fair-sized house . . . $7,500." There is a strong tradition in the family that Jack was the first motorist in Ontario to make a long-distance trip; he drove his own car the 140 or more miles from Toronto to Muskoka on a summer day in the early 1900's, plotting his course from one dirt road to the next, and carrying complete equipment for refuelling and repairs.

Like all rich men he went through a yachting phase. First, there was the schooner *Tekla*, ninety-four feet long and fitted with wireless which could exchange business messages with an elaborate installation on the store roof – the first service of the kind in Toronto. As the years went by, there was a succession of steam yachts, culminating in the famous *Florence* which he purchased in New York and, with a crew of eighteen and his family aboard, brought to its Toronto berth by way of a very choppy sea and the Gulf of St Lawrence. The Commodore and members of the Royal Canadian Yacht Club lined up in a gay welcoming flotilla on Toronto Bay as the *Florence* appeared on the horizon, and even the old ferry "tubs" joined in the hubbub with throaty salutes to the gleaming white ship, handsomest creature of her kind ever to enter the local waters. Luxurious travel was Jack Eaton's delight, especially if he had his friends along to share it. His private railway car, the *Eatonia*, which he had ordered for his father's use, frequently became Jack's family headquarters, and office too, on transcontinental trips.

For his wife's first visit to Europe, it was decided that they would take passage in the sumptuous new liner, the *Lusitania.* Jack talked up the project among his friends, with the result that the final Eaton party to file across the gangplank in New York numbered eleven. It was an unforgettable holiday; their hearts were young and gay, and their zest for the new experience, whether in a mediæval Swiss *schloss* or along the Paris boulevards or driving in an open car through English fog, boundless. Ireland was the last point on the itinerary, and together the two descendants of Ulster forefathers made a sentimental pilgrimage to the places they had heard about since cradle days – the Glens of Antrim, Ballymena, Belfast.

By 1910 it was obvious that the cosy Walmer Road house had become inadequate for the Eatons' needs. There were now two sons, seven-year-old Timothy and John David, born October 4, 1909. The busy household required a staff of three maids, and the guestrooms were seldom unoccupied. A big house was clearly indicated, and Jack plunged into the enterprise with the same enthusiasm as for the Winnipeg Store. A semi-country estate rising up Toronto's "Hill" on the north side of Davenport Road was acquired, the existing structures demolished, and the excitement of planning began. The place had to live up to its new name, *Ardwold*, an Irish term signifying "high on a green hill," and every advantage must be taken of the magnificent view over city and distant lake. "Not only have you a splendid view," said one of the architects, standing on the crest with the new owners, "but just imagine being able to look out at 300,000 people who work for you!" Jack chided him for the slight exaggeration.

While the construction was underway, Flora and the children joined a larger family party for a leisurely visit abroad and, although Jack's letters reported rapid progress, she was hardly prepared for a *fait accompli* on her return. Driving up from the Union Station, Jack turned to her casually and said, "We'll just go and have a look at *Ardwold*, so you can see how it's getting on." They did, and not only was it almost finished, but every piece of furniture, every cup and saucer from the Walmer Road house had been moved in, and she would never again step across the threshold of her first Toronto home. Probably her state of shock was contagious, for two-year-old John David burst into tears and cried, "I don't like this ho-tel . . . I want to go home!"

But *Ardwold*, huge as it was with its fifty rooms, fourteen bathrooms, and its half-acre of glassed-over section for swimming pool and conservatories, graciously submitted to domestication. All the Eatons today remember it with affection – and to many Torontonians "The Hill" has never looked quite the same since the great house was torn down some twenty years ago to make way for new streets.

Its exact cost has been forgotten, but ten years after completion *Ardwold* was valued for estate purposes at $300,000. The building was of Georgian design in buff brick with stone trim. The many windows of the south façade captured sun and view for the main rooms and two bedroom floors above; centred on the roof was a crown-like structure, the "lantern" room from which the panorama of city, lake, and sky, especially at sunset, was quite breathtaking. Inside, the core of the plan was the great hall, two storeys high, with an open gallery supported by arches; the massive staircase rose from one end of the room, and facing it was the stone fireplace. The mellow gleam of panelling and decorative carving, done by a leading Italian craftsman, gave both warmth and richness to the setting. Here, family and guests would gather after dinner, especially when Jack was present to play a few selections on the mechanical Aeolian pipe organ. This was his favourite evening diversion; over the years he assembled a fine library of the special recordings, done on perforated paper rolls, and he delighted in studying the best effects with the various organ-stops and volume adjustments.

Ardwold was unique in its provision, on the third floor, of a small hospital with two bedrooms and bathroom for patients, a white-tiled surgery with sterilizing and spraying equipment, and a small washing-up room for a doctor's use. One major operation and many minor ones were performed there, but the suite's main purpose was to isolate any member of the household suffering from a communicable disease. Another feature was the large nursery section with its own small kitchen and dining-room. Staff and service quarters occupied a three-storey wing which gave the house its L-shape.

No one ever claimed that *Ardwold* was the largest house in Toronto, for by the time it was fully functioning all such superlatives belonged to its near neighbour, *Casa Loma*, the neo-feudal dream-child of Sir Henry Pellatt. Many pleasant visits were exchanged between *Ardwold* and the castle, and the Eatons were always to remember that it was through the friendly interest of Sir Henry that they found their farm, northwest of Toronto at King, where *Eaton Hall* would one day be built as successor to *Ardwold* in the line of clan headquarters.

Without the family and the Company, without *Ardwold* and its hospitality, Toronto's war effort from 1914 to 1918 would certainly have been different and undoubtedly less.

Eaton's had been part of Canadian history long enough to have stored up memories of two previous campaigns that had involved some of their own men. In 1885 six or seven employees volunteered to serve with the local regiments sent to the far northwest to take Louis Riel and his rebels. In the South African War four men of the Eaton staff shipped out with the Canadian contingent; full wages were paid to them during their absence, and on their return a triumphant welcome was given them at Massey Hall where gold watches were presented by Mrs Timothy Eaton.

Now, in the hot summer of 1914, Canada was committed to a totally modern war.

A few days after the official declaration from Ottawa, the Eaton President and his directors announced their plans to aid recruitment. Any married employee volunteering for service would receive full pay for the duration, and any single man half-pay. (By October 1919 these military service allowances had reached the sum of $2,206,443, paid to a total of 3,327 Eaton employees from the Toronto and Winnipeg organizations.)

Another important decision was that in any war contracts received by the firm (and there were to be very large orders for army clothing and leather equipment, and so on), all profits would be returned to the government.

Within a few months, when it was apparent that the new weapon called the machine gun would be a vital factor in this war, Jack Eaton presented his personal cheque for $100,000 to equip what was soon to be known as the Eaton Machine Gun Battery with Vickers-Maxim guns mounted on fifteen armoured trucks.

The yacht *Florence* was turned over to the government; after a year of patrol service she was lost off Trinidad, assumed to be the victim of enemy action.

The President became one of the prime movers in the Patriotic Fund, and this, plus his efforts on behalf of soldiers' dependants, grew into an almost full-time job as the war continued.

Ardwold provided the setting for innumerable wartime charity events; its guest suites and dining-room were constantly filled with visitors, many of them servicemen. The vast house was being utilized to capacity, from the third-floor nursery – now the domain of two more sons, Edgar Allison, born in 1912, and Gilbert McCrea, three years younger – to the big kitchens where sometimes whole banquets were prepared for dispatching to military hospital or barracks. Flora's attractive music room did service for committee meetings from time to time as her West Toronto women's patriotic group increased in numbers and skills for the production of soldiers' comforts and hospital supplies.

The war brought public honours to the family and the firm with the conferring of a knighthood on John Craig Eaton in recognition of his outstanding contributions to his country's cause. The investiture at Rideau Hall, to which Mr and Mrs Jack Eaton were "commanded" in the autumn of 1915, was to go down as one of the solemnly wonderful events in their shared experiences. The King's representative was himself Royalty, H.R.H. the Duke of Connaught, and the ancient ritual lost nothing in the hands of this son of Queen Victoria. When Jack's name was called, he walked forward, knelt in front of the Duke who touched him on each shoulder with his sword and uttered the words, "Arise, Sir Knight . . . . " Flora could hardly restrain her tears of pride and happiness.

Following the ceremony, luncheon was served at three round tables, each of which was presided over by a Connaught. Sir John was seated beside Princess Patricia; his wife joined the Duchess's table. And it was interesting for them both to discover that the constantly repeated rumour about Royal meals and the rule of a one-hour maximum time allowance was indeed true; several guests who innocently laid down knife and fork for a moment were obviously astounded when the footman whisked their unfinished course away.

The war had brought the Eatons a conspicuous honour; in the same year, 1915, it had plunged them into tragedy as well. Sir John's sister, Mrs Burnside, and her twenty-year-old daughter Iris were travelling to England in the *Lusitania*; four Eaton managers were passengers too; and of that group of relatives and friends only Josie survived after the torpedoing of the ship off the coast of Ireland. A year or so later Tom Eaton, son of old Uncle James's second marriage and a popular junior executive in the Toronto store, was to be killed in action in France. The President's brother, Colonel Bill Eaton, spent several years in uniform as Assistant Director of Recruiting for Canada and in other army posts in Ottawa.

It was the First Great War which added a famous new name to the Eaton connection: none other than the brilliant young Canadian fighter ace, Billy Bishop, winner of the V.C. and every other military decoration the King could bestow. Bishop, comrade of another distinguished war pilot, Henry J. Burden, came back to Canada on leave in 1917, fell in love with his friend's sister, Margaret Burden, and there was a wedding such as Toronto had never witnessed before. "The love of the world for a fair young bride and her hero bridegroom," as one of the society editors reported it, was demonstrated by milling thousands of people around Timothy Eaton Memorial Church; inside, the pews were crammed to the topmost gallery row. It was a glorious family occasion, and today two middle-aged men enjoy an occasional reminiscence about their expert service as Cousin Margaret's train-bearers: Noel Eaton, son of Colonel Bill, and John David. Admittedly the assignment had its challenging aspects for the two eight-year-olds. "We were gussied up in blue velvet suits with lace collars," Noel recalls, "and we had tricorne hats to match. Just imagine trying to walk slow and stay in step and keep a three-cornered hat under one arm and hang onto a satin train with both hands – while all those people watched!"

The Eatons, of course, have always been "watched" and talked about. Mostly they accept the situation good-naturedly, and often the family has a round of hilarity over the latest gossip. If the story has to do with the Company and seems to be disturbing their associates, the Eatons have been known to speak out plainly. Shortly after Timothy Eaton's death there had been a rumour that the new President contemplated "selling out" (occasionally it circulated with the extra tag, "to an American group"), and its stubborn persistence finally prodded one of the department heads to bring up the subject at a managers' conference. The matter was closed, satisfactorily and forever, by one simple statement from John Craig Eaton. "There is not enough money in the whole world to buy my father's name," he said, and then turned to the morning's agenda.

Titles are rare enough in Canada to make their holders fair game for idle chatter, and doubtless the stories multiplied after the conferring of the Eaton knighthood. At any rate, it was during that period when Sir John actually did rise up in wrath. He was returning on the regular night train from Montreal and had sauntered into the smoker to finish his cigar before going to bed. Two men were sitting there, and one began a dissertation on the Eatons, pretending very special knowledge concerning the business, the family, and in particular the President and his wife. Sir John reached in his pocket for his card case and stood up. "Here is my card, sir," he said, "and I want you to know that everything you have been saying is a damned lie!"

There was a good deal of whispering when Edward Johnson, the brilliant Canadian-born opera star, became an intimate of the Eaton circle, and the comments became noisier following the announcement that Lady Eaton would sing on the same program with him in Massey Hall. She had kept up her music studies more or less continuously over the years, occasionally joined with other advanced students in recitals, and enjoyed singing for small groups in her own home. But Johnson was world-famous and the darling of New York's Metropolitan Opera! So Toronto had a field day for gossip. . . . "What cheek she has!"; "There's more in this than meets the eye"; "It'll cost her husband a pretty penny – and he probably engineered the whole thing."

Actually it was Edward Johnson who had proposed the scheme: if she would share a concert with him he would donate his services, and all monies received from the sale of tickets could be turned over to any of her charities. She pleaded home duties – the Eatons' new baby and first daughter, Florence Mary, was just five months old, having been born on November 15, 1919 – and there seemed little time to rehearse. But Sir John wore down her protests, and so did the Lieutenant-Governor's wife whose Canadian National Institute for the Blind would be the beneficiary, and eventually the gala evening arrived. Lady Eaton was a majestic, glittering figure in her blue-and-silver brocade gown with train, wearing a tiara, ropes of pearls, and the good-luck bracelet her husband had given her just a few hours previous: platinum with the first bar of her first song picked out in black enamel and diamonds. Strangely enough, it was the professional rather than the amateur who was nervous; he confessed he always underwent tension quivers before going on stage. But the occasion was entirely successful, and after that first experience Lady Eaton accepted various invitations to participate in important musical events, notably with the local symphony orchestra.

"Eduardo," as the Eatons called Edward Johnson, was to hold a special place among the family for the rest of his life. When his engagements permitted, he was with them in Toronto or Muskoka (once, with his daughter, now Mrs George Drew, he spent a summer at the lake, rehearsing for his next opera season). If "The Court," (as one of Lady Eaton's relatives dubbed her entourage of children, governess, chauffeur, nursemaid) was on the move to New York or London or Italy, Eduardo made an effort to be in attendance if possible.

The history of the Eaton family from the 1920's onward is threaded through with the sparkle of the gay, romantic devotion which Edward Johnson delighted to give.

Far back at the beginning of the century, Timothy Eaton had made a prophetic remark before a gathering of his workers. "I may not live to see it," he said, "but some of you younger men, I believe, will see the time when the world's business can be done in five working-days, and better done than in six, and when Saturday will be given up entirely to recreation, and Sunday to rest and worship."

His youngest son was never to lose sight of that hope. In 1919, as a tribute to the war effort of Eaton personnel and also in celebration of the Company's Golden Jubilee year, Sir John announced the full Saturday holiday during July and August, and the half-holiday for the rest of the year. It was a revolutionary step in the retailing world, and a pioneering of the way for the gradual adoption of the five-day week throughout Canadian industry and commerce. Nowadays Eaton stores in the big cities are open six days a week and generally one or two evenings as well, but each employee works on a five-day-week basis.

As soon as word of Sir John's plan went round the store, the employees set about making their own reciprocal tribute. The sum of $20,000 was collected and given in the President's name to the Hospital for Sick Children for extensions to the X-ray wing and the endowment of a cot. At a huge Golden Jubilee rally of

Eatonians in Toronto's Armouries, Sir John, following the cheers that welcomed his official proclamation of the new hours, was asked to accept his employees' gift; he was not only surprised but visibly moved – for any project designed to help the sick or needy was close to his heart.

Of the estimated $4,000,000 of his public benefactions, upwards of $500,000 had gone to establish the Sir John and Lady Eaton chair in medicine at the University of Toronto, and another $365,000 contributed the Surgical Wing of the Toronto General Hospital. The list of his $50,000 gifts to colleges, church campaigns, the Navy League, the Royal Ontario Museum, and other projects becomes almost monotonous reading. When a serious emergency faced the nation he could be counted upon as one of the first citizens to take action. Within an hour of the news of the Halifax explosion – in December 1917, when two ships, one loaded with TNT, rammed in the harbour and spread fire, death, and chaos over a large area – Sir John had alerted the store's chief pharmacist and *Ardwold's* two trained nurses to form a team; together they assembled blankets, clothing, foodstuffs, and medical supplies, packed them into the *Eatonia* and a full-size freight car, and by the next day the expedition was on its way with the regular fast train to Halifax, where the group, headed by the President, spent one week.

Yet these public acts of sympathetic, practical giving are far from the whole story of his generosity. For years he retained one of the local legal firms for the sole purpose of handling his private gifts, many of them made anonymously, to struggling families trying to pay off a mortgage, old employees confronted with misfortune, or talented young people forced to drop their final education and training because of a shortage of funds. Friends close to him estimated that possibly another half-million dollars was channelled in this way.

When he died at *Ardwold* at the end of March 1922, as the result of pneumonia following flu, Sir John Craig Eaton was just forty-six years of age, and no doubt still far from the realization of his full potential. But in the memory of those who worked for him and with him, he was to remain forever young, forever the buoyant character who wanted to share his happiness with everyone. The remark, made so often among the thousands of mourners who passed by his bier in an endless line, is still heard today: "There was only one Jack – a prince among men!"

PART
THREE

A Cousin in Command

PART THREE

Eaton's has had just four presidents during its 94-year history, and each of them has been a man of and for his own era. Timothy Eaton, the founder, typified the nineteenth century's Horatio Alger hero, doggedly confident in the rewards both on earth and in heaven for the applied virtues of diligence, honesty, and Christian charity. Next came Sir John Craig Eaton, perfectly matched to his Edwardian hour: a gregarious figure, effortlessly accumulating friends and legends as he moved through his rounds of duties, giving lavishly in public or private on a scale never before witnessed in Canada. His son, John David Eaton, head of the vastly greater merchandising empire which is Eaton's of Canada today, is the new-style multi-millionaire dedicated to the study of the world and the welfare state in which business is conducted; a reader, a level-eyed listener rather than a talker; shy of society and its gushy occasions; uncompromising in decisions carefully arrived at.

Between Sir John's death and his son's assumption of office, there occurred, not exactly an interregnum, not quite a regency, but a "holding" presidency which was to cover a highly important period in both store and family history. This break in the direct succession was necessitated by the fact that Sir John's four sons and one daughter were much too young to inherit (John David, the second child, was in his thirteenth year at the time of his father's death), and also by the instructions in the will, which directed that his Company stock be kept intact until one of the children, selected by the executors for character and business ability, would be ready to take over.

So for the next twenty years – while the main-line descendants grew up, went to school, and eventually found their footholds in Company jobs – an interim president was in charge. His name was Robert Young Eaton, "R. Y.," Sir John's cousin and First Vice-President, a devoutly conscientious Eaton at all times yet totally different from his predecessors. Perhaps one of the reasons might be traced to his rather late indoctrination in things and ways Canadian, for he was the last of the numerous Eatons to leave their native Antrim. Circumstances were such, however, that he had become a hard-working Eatonian by the time he had his first look at Toronto.

R. Y. was the youngest surviving child born to Timothy's brother John, the stay-at-home Eaton who by dint of his own efforts (aided by Gladstone's Irish land-reform measures) rose from a small tenant farmer to the position of country gentleman. He eventually became the owner of *Ahoghill*, a considerable estate near Ballymena, an employer of labour, and a man constantly active in advancing rural education for Northern Ireland. One by one, John's adult children had emigrated – all to Canada, with the exception of a daughter who married a United States citizen, John St Clair, and finally settled in California. The first to arrive on the Toronto scene was William Herbinson Eaton, a youth in his 'teens; Uncle Timothy employed and watched over him for some years, but "Herby" grew restless under the careful training and finally left for Selkirk, Manitoba, where he opened a small store. He had already received glowing accounts of that pioneer prairie community from his brother John James – one of the few Eatons who never, at any period of their lifetime, had behind-the-counter contact with mercantile operations. The John Jameses, father and sons, made their living on the open plains with their horses which they bred and trained; their descendants were to expand the tradition with popular rodeo displays across the western provinces.

At the time of the *Ahoghill* owner's death, young R. Y. was the sole survivor at home. Nevertheless, the lad had been marked out for a career quite different from farming, or the civil service which he now planned to enter. Uncle Timothy on his frequent visits had been impressed with Bob's astuteness as to crops and farm maintenance and the management of hired hands. That sort of careful efficiency could be useful in retailing, too, and in 1897 Bob was persuaded to say goodbye to Antrim and go direct to the London buying-office of the T. Eaton Co. His first job was shipping-clerk, and when he rolled down his shirtsleeves at the end of the working-day he generally faced another four hours of active concentration on his "grinder" course at the University of London. A few years later he was moved to the Paris office, and in 1902, at the age of twenty-seven, he was summoned to Canada to assume the duties of Secretary of the Company.

Several of Bob's unmarried sisters were already settled in Toronto and there was a great reunion when their adored little brother, six-foot-five and broad of frame, moved in with them and unpacked his belongings, including the old violin of *Ahoghill* days. For the next few years their modest house – five minutes' walk from Uncle Timothy's mansion – constituted still another family stronghold, often lively with visitors, sometimes deserted by weekend expeditions to Eaton relatives out of town. R. Y. became an indefatigable keeper-in-touch. On his first trip to the prairies he looked up his brothers and their families, and from that visit sprang the interesting rumour of later years that one of his new-found relatives was a beautiful Indian girl. Closer at hand there were many Eaton cousins to call on: the Reids in Georgetown, the Youngs in London and St Marys, the current Crabbe generation in Toronto. Whereas Uncle Timothy and his family gradually let these contacts lapse, R. Y. and his sisters maintained an interest in the whole connection and gathered a certain popularity as a result. It was among the Youngs (Nancy Eaton Young's group in western Ontario) that the big fellow with the grass-green Antrim accent got his nickname of "Irish Bob," as a means of distinguishing him from the Canadian-born cousin, Robert Wellington Eaton.

At the store he was always "Mr R. Y.," of course, and always on the way up. By 1911 he was securely established as First Vice-President, and so immersed in Company operation, so little diverted by pretty girls, that observers prophesied he would stay a bachelor for life. But that was the year he met Hazel Margaret Ireland in her home town of Carberry, Manitoba, and after a big church wedding the following December, still another charming bride of an Eaton was facing the overwhelming warmth of a family welcome to Toronto.

She was not quite twenty-three years old – thirteen years younger than her husband – but already she had won Carberry's admiration as the able organist and choir leader at Knox Presbyterian Church, and one of the best piano-teachers in the Brandon-Carberry district. Her student years at the Toronto Conservatory of Music, where she graduated with an ATCM, had given her pleasant memories of the city and its famous store. And so far as the Eatons were concerned, she was in the best tradition of a senior executive's wife: gentle in manner, congenial in any group, and of sound Irish ancestry through her father, a respected businessman who had been Carberry's first mayor.

She was striking in appearance, too, with luminous big brown eyes, quantities of rich dark hair, creamy skin, and a brilliant smile. Her good looks and neat figure continued far past middle age, and for many years the entrance of the R. Y. Eatons at an evening function would inspire whispers from the sidelines: "She's so attractive, isn't she!"

But no similar handy phrase was ever hit upon to sum up her husband, and even to this day, though there are countless Company anecdotes to draw upon, his personality resists easy analysis. He had few intimates, no cronies, or boon companions; if he relaxed at all, it was at home, yet even there the responsibilities of being a good father and disciplinarian to five vigorous children demanded constant alertness. Indeed, discipline and preparedness were the *leit-motifs* of all R. Y.'s activities; for him there could be little enjoyment of the present moment unless one took all precautions against the uncertainties of the next.

By the time he assumed the presidency in 1922 he had an encyclopædic knowledge of every phase of Company business. His head was a filing cabinet of figures to the last decimal point; department executives quickly learned never to quote an approximate sum of costs or profits in his presence. He became his own perambulating suggestion box as he made his frequent rounds. He liked to stand for a while in Mattresses or China, watching the triumphant final act of merchandising; he seemed unaware of his conspicuousness, but every clerk knew this towering mountain of a man with the unsmiling face and balding dome, and anybody passing close by would hear the tuneless, toneless whistle which was his fixed habit, whether alone or in conversation. After such inspection visits the managers could expect a little hand-written note suggesting improvements in displays or the conduct of personnel. R. Y. was the first and only Eaton president who enjoyed writing memos, and there are dozens of these wisps of neatly pencilled comments tucked away in odd corners throughout the organization. Some, surprisingly, reveal an ingrained feeling for the romance of the organization he headed as, for instance, when he wrote to the senior woman writer in City Advertising, who had submitted a draft outline for a booklet: "Cannot imagination run riot as one thinks of Madam Canada sitting snugly by her fireside, while in far Japan the Eaton Buyers, Toronto & Winnipeg men, are reaching out of the way places for silks, kimonos and crockery that she may be able to see these products in her own store. . . . Madam Toronto may in an afternoon walk through her favourite shopping place, see & compare the products of every country of the old world and the new, welcome to ask questions, to be shown gladly but no importunity to buy. . . . And to do it in a way that no one is obliged to keep anything that he does not want to keep?"

A great many things were to happen during the R. Y. régime, and one of the first owed its initiating impulse, and indeed final achievement, to Lady Eaton. She had been made a director by her husband in 1921; now she was a very active Vice-President, and in many ways the wide-awake conscience and prodder of Eaton management in the field of employee relations. Her deep conviction that all workers should have an opportunity to see, meet, and when possible chat with their Eaton employers, and that a staff's personal goodwill and confidence constituted a primary Company asset, had led her into an annual undertaking that is still talked about when Eaton old-timers get together. Once a year she visited every Eaton building in Canada, whether factory or store or Mail Order; the routine was to take the elevator to the top floor and then walk down, progressing unhurriedly through each department, noting the arrangements, whether shabby or neat, the employees' restrooms, lunch facilities, and so on, and stopping to exchange a pleasant word or two here and there. Her frank reports and recommendations are now locked away in the Board's archives, but the results of them, and their updated improvements, are still in evidence in countless ways.

One morning she astounded the gentlemen around the boardroom table by telling them that Eaton's needed a completely new, fine restaurant service, of the type to appeal to discriminating women. Her colleagues listened attentively as she warmed to the subject, but they were not persuaded; the plan, they said, would be too costly and actually wasn't "a business proposition." Very well, came back Lady Eaton, she would accept their decision, "but I have one favour to ask. I want you to close down the restaurant we now have, for I am ashamed of it."

That afternoon R. Y., after some further thought, hastened to *Ardwold* to reopen the matter, and within hours the Vice-President and one other director were appointed a committee for action. Their meetings began next day; soon Lady Eaton had engaged the brilliant dietician who would direct the enterprise; in a few months, construction crews swarmed over the huge new floor thrust up over the main store; and in 1924 the Georgian Room was ready to serve the public, and incidentally to provide a brisk fillip for restaurant standards in Toronto and even beyond. By the end of its first year the venture had amply proved its worth as "a business proposition"; the directors were well content as they sat at their own table in the far corner every lunchtime and swept their eyes over the bobbing sea of women's hats, the lines of tables gleaming with pretty china, silver, and glass (the same patterns, so carefully selected by the two ladies, are still in use today), and the waitresses' trays in full bloom with that Georgian Room creation called "salad plates." It was obvious that a dining-service of this character would henceforth be an essential feature in all Eaton's big-city establishments.

At the moment, several such were underway or in the discussion stage. By 1925 the Montreal store had opened; within the next few years there were to be others in Hamilton and Halifax and in Moncton, where a Mail Order headquarters for the Maritimes had been in busy operation for some years. The purchase of the Canadian Department Stores, a retailing network in smaller centres, was a significant event, another portent of the "Eaton's of Canada" coverage in the far-off future. And soon the great College Street Store in Toronto – which had been one of Sir John's dearest dreams but which he had firmly set aside in 1914 "until we win this war," as he said – would start to take shape.

Far back when the property had been acquired, the plan had been to move Eaton's *in toto* from the old downtown location; but by the time building could be commenced there were significant new factors which would alter that scheme. For one thing, there was a constantly increasing population of women in jobs – and these noon-hour customers from the office buildings might find it too much to make the mile trip north to College Street. Moreover, Simpson's expanding competition just across the road from Eaton's main store was not to be lightly written off, nor the habit of several generations of Toronto women to visit both the department stores on every shopping-trip. Construction costs had risen enormously as well. Yet a new building was desperately needed, if only for the booming furniture departments.

So the eventual structure reflected all these considerations in its final size and sections. At the Yonge and College corner rose the main part of the imposing seven-storey building, which was given over chiefly to house furnishings; to the south and to the west stretched low wings for various specialty departments. The all-important restaurant took the form and name of the Round Room, decorated in discreet contemporary style by a leading artist brought from Paris; across the way from it on the seventh floor was R. Y. Eaton's special pride and joy: the Eaton Auditorium, complete with stage and pipe-organ and large audience capacity. When the President handed the key to his newly appointed Auditorium manager, a cryptic R. Y. remark went with it. "The audiences that come are to wear formal evening dress," he said. That was the sole clue to the Auditorium's future, yet it sufficed. From that point forward the great names in music – Flagstad, Lily Pons, Schnabel, the rest – were regularly booked, and Toronto people were glad to pay the price, both in season tickets and fine raiment, to attend.

Eaton's–College Street has sometimes been described as "the crown jewel" in the Company chain; retailers from abroad have declared it one of the beautiful mercantile establishments of the world. Certainly, when it opened, Toronto people turned out by the tens of thousands to make the tour of its spacious floors, admire the all-Canadian materials and workmanship (ivory Tyndall limestone from Manitoba, black granite from Mount Johnson, Quebec, brown granite from Gananoque, Ontario), gaze in awe at the series of sumptuously decorated period rooms, ride in the elevators, and then leave without buying. For it was the fate of Eaton's–College Street to open in October 1930, about eleven months after the crash of stock-exchange prices which triggered the Depression. Years would pass before the millions of dollars invested in the new store would begin to pay off. All Eaton outlets were to suffer, each in its own way and according to area, as Canada's national employment slowed and average income dropped by 45 per cent (farmers' by 70 per cent), and business failures became a commonplace in the news of the day.

The anxieties expressed around Eaton's boardroom table week by week through the early 'thirties can only be imagined, for they have never been revealed. But so far as the Company's public image was concerned, it stayed undiminished. Mr R. Y. was proving himself the man for his hour – cautious, steady, impossible to panic. At times he tried to share his confidence with the community through special Eaton advertisements. The day before Christmas 1930, cordial thanks to customers and employees were conveyed, followed by this statement: "We are pleased to be able to report that in city business we have delivered more parcels than ever before, and, besides, we have actually working in the Toronto store(s), mail order and factory the largest staff we have ever had in the history of the Company." One year later, the same sort of message included the significant line: "Our aisles filled with busy buying crowds was [*sic*] in these days a cheering sight for all." In early 1933, large-space advertisements under the heading, "How Employment is Created," offered a readable lesson in elementary economics, listed some of the 278 Ontario centres which had had a share of Eaton purchases in the preceding year (Peterborough, $413,000; Kitchener, $1,130,000, and so on), and reminded the public that Eaton's policy had always been for "small profits and greater volume" for the benefit of producers, consumers, and all the workers involved, including the Company's own payroll.

It was a routine Eaton advertisement, however, that would suddenly receive national attention in the House of Commons. The Bennett government, desperate to find causes and causers of the economic slump, pounced on the morning-paper message that curtain nets could be had for the lowest price ever, because of the size of the order placed by Eaton's buyer in Britain. While Toronto housewives were eagerly on their way downtown to investigate the bargain, Parliament debated the morals of mass buying at low prices, and out of this harangue was finally to emerge the Price Spreads Committee of 1934 when various leading manufacturers and retailers would be summoned to appear in Ottawa. The T. Eaton Co. retained the brilliant economist, Professor Gilbert Jackson, to prepare and present its brief, and he was able to prove – to the satisfaction of most of the politicians and newspaper commentators alike – that out of each customer's dollar received at the counter over the past five years, 76.3 cents went into the actual cost of the merchandise to the Company; profit and interest on borrowings combined amounted to 2 cents; and the balance, just under 22 cents, was paid out in wages and other merchandising services. The Canadian Press summary continued: "Further, comparing the Eaton Company's gross margin between cost and selling price with the equivalent figures for 317 department and 48 specialty stores in the United States, Prof. Jackson revealed that the Canadian firm's highest gross margin for three years (26.3% in 1932) was narrower than the narrowest among the American groups during the same three years."

The crisis, along with the government which precipitated it, soon subsided into history; but it is remembered today as possibly the single important occasion in almost a century of operation when the

Company was subjected to the harsh glare of a national investigation.

Although R. Y. had the deepest veneration for his Uncle Timothy's principles and methods, he showed himself sufficiently flexible to move with the times. Until his presidency the only alternative to a cash deal was the deposit account system: an advance payment plan whereby a customer banked her shopping money with Eaton's, received interest, and had her purchases debited against the sum on deposit. In the 'twenties, when the public surge into the motor car market had made instalment-buying eminently respectable, Eaton's introduced the deferred payment plan; customers were invited to try a buy-now pay-later arrangement for certain large-scale purchases. The success of the scheme (and even through the worst of the hard-time years there were remarkably few defaulters) led to further refinements and eventually to charge accounts. Today a customer has several choices for the financing of her fur coat or her broadloom. The only method not open to her is old-time barter: Timothy's determined stand against accepting a tub of country butter in exchange for a length of dress goods is still unalterable Company policy.

Employees' welfare and recreation projects were never allowed to lapse, whether the times were good or bad. Hospital care, home nursing service and sick-pay allowance were extended during the R. Y. period. A female clerk in the Toronto store could spend her vacation at the Eaton Girls' Club camp at Shadow Lake for about three dollars a week. The big community athletic events started by Sir John years before – often featuring world-famous stars and drawing crowds of fifteen thousand spectators – had been replaced by participating sportsmen's groups within the Company. And for everybody interested and sufficiently skilled, such organizations as the Eaton Camera Club and the Eaton Operatic Society held out the added attraction of an occasional gala evening at the President's residence, *Killyree* (named after his birthplace). The big music room, capable of holding well over a hundred guests, was the setting, and sometimes the entertainment included a few piano numbers by Mrs R. Y.

The house in Toronto, the summer place on a Georgian Bay island, the farm at Port Credit, the stable of fine hunters – all these allowed for a busy rotation of activities for R. Y.'s family. The children had inherited their mother's glowing good looks and their father's love of tennis and horses; for years there was seldom a major horse show in Canada, New York, London, or Ireland without one of these Eatons – twins Jack and Margaret, Erskine, Alan, Nora – in the jumping competitions with a well-trained mount from the home stables.

It was R. Y.'s interest in horses that led him to accept the appointment of Honorary Colonel of the Governor General's Horse Guards; by the time the regiment converted to armour he had become a keen military man, and no one was surprised when all three sons and one daughter chose the army for their service in the Second World War. The death of Lieutenant Erskine Eaton, killed in action in 1942, removed the undoubted charmer of the group, but immediately it seemed as if, in the words of one observer, "the family gritted their teeth all the harder to win the war." Margaret shut the door firmly on her wardrobe of pretty clothes and signed on with the Canadian Women's Army Corps; within a short time she rose to the rank of Lieutenant-Colonel and proved herself a recruiting dynamo in the Toronto area. Today she and her doctor-husband make their home in London, England. Nora's marriage took her to permanent residence in the United States. Their two brothers are firmly established in the higher echelons of the Eaton organization; both are Directors, with Jack W. the General Manager of Eaton's Quebec Department Store Division, and Alan Y. the Company Controller at head office in Toronto. The latter has served several terms as President of the Art Gallery of Toronto – an office which his father held for many years.

When R. Y.'s presidency drew to a close, there were probably numerous sighs of relief at many Eaton points across the country. He was a man sometimes feared, seldom loved, always respected. "But in business it is better to be respected than loved," is the quick comment of his sister Emily, an active lady of ninety and the last of the Eaton-born members of her generation. That R. Y. himself was cognizant of his status with business associates is shown by one little conversational clash.

Persons, Places, and Occasions

Today's President, John David Eaton, and his mother, Lady Eaton, stand in front of Timothy Eaton's statue, which, from its position against the Yonge Street side of the Toronto store's main floor, overlooks one of Canada's busiest retailing areas

In Portglenone, County Antrim: the building where young Tim served his toilsome years as storekeeper's apprentice

Clogher Farm, near Ballymena – birthplace of many Eatons, including Timothy. Buildings still stand in 1963

Timothy Eaton, photographed in Toronto shortly after he had opened his store there in 1869, at the age of 35

R. Y. Eaton, 1922-42 President, on happy holiday at Georgian Bay in his later years; his wife beside him

Ardwold's south front, overlooking the city of Toronto. Lantern structure on roof was a fair-sized sitting-room

Sir John Craig Eaton in an informal snapshot taken a year or so before his death in 1922 at the age of forty-six

Ardwold's Great Hall, rising more than two storeys and gleaming with rich panelling, was a favourite after-dinner gathering place – especially when Sir John was present to operate the Aeolian mechanical pipe-organ

The Timothy Eatons' big house, about a mile south of *Ardwold*, maintained an ebullient late Victorian atmosphere throughout its long career as a family mansion. Here, a view of drawing-room from archway of main hall

1962: At Timothy Eaton Memorial Church, the new Flora McCrea Eaton Building, gift of President and his wife

1913: Cornerstone ceremony for the Timothy Eaton Memorial Church. Mrs Eaton with son Jack nearby

1901: Jack Eaton at the wheel drives the future King George V (*rear, left*) on a sightseeing tour of Toronto

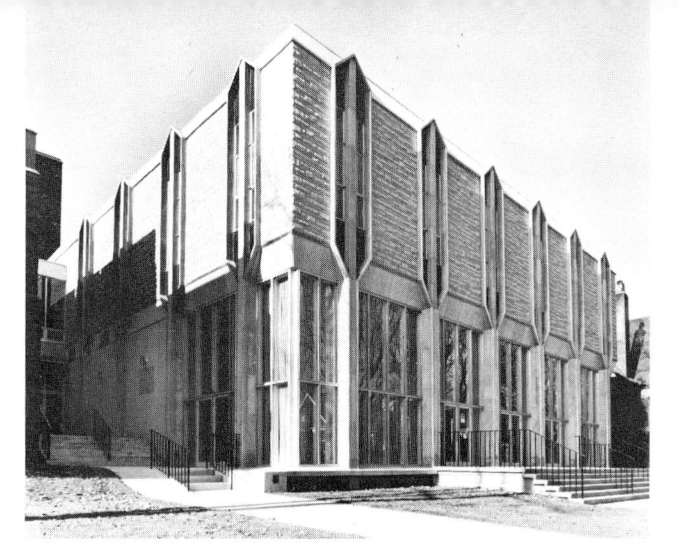

The Santa Claus Parade – a fixture in the Eaton calendar for more than half a century. Winnipeg, 1908, cheered these horse-drawn floats. Modern Toronto loves its big occasion, as indicated; later, thousands rush into store to watch the jolly old fellow mount his throne

WELCOME TO EATON'S TOYLAND

Two panoramic glimpses of today's main family headquarters: *Eaton Hall* at King, near Toronto. The occasion was the 1946 welcome-home party given by the President and Directors to all Eaton war veterans in the Ontario area

Windows and terrace on the south side of the house command a broad sweep of lawn and gardens and the beautiful sheet of water called Lake Jonda. On opposite shore is picnic centre with barbecue, wading pool, diving tower

1933: *Kawandag*'s gardens, plus a blue Muskoka sky, supplied the setting for the wedding of Signy Hilda Stefasson of Winnipeg to John David Eaton, second son of Sir John

1958: Mr and Mrs John David Eaton and family, photographed in their Toronto home. *The sons, from left:* Fredrik Stefan, Thor Edgar, George Ross, John Craig II

1929: Lady Eaton and family at *Kawandag*, the Muskoka residence. *Seated, from left:* John David, Florence Mary, Evlyn Beatrice, Edgar Allison. *Standing:* Gilbert McCrea, Lady Eaton, and eldest son, Timothy

Four generations caught by a family camera on Christmas day at *Eaton Hall.* John David Eaton is at left; his first grandchild and namesake sits on Lady Eaton's lap; his eldest son, John Craig II, looks proudly happy in the rôle of young father. The day's program always includes carol singing, distribution of gifts from a huge tree by a costumed Santa Claus, and dinner for all ages, except infants, in the big dining-room. A private Communion service at the *Hall* opens the family's Christmas week.

It took place during a presidential visit to an Eaton factory. The manager, a younger Eaton, was attempting to save the job of a certain employee who had been discovered in a serious mistake. R. Y. insisted on nothing less than discharge; the manager, after using all the soft means of persuasion, finally spoke out loud and clear, "Cousin Bob, why do you have to be so hard to get along with?"

The big man stopped his whistling long enough to make what was, for him, a major statement. "When you own a business yourself, it is easy to be lenient, to grant largesse and to be popular with everyone. When you have been given the responsibility of running a business *in trust* for someone else, it is a different matter."

PART FOUR

The Eaton Empire Today

PART FOUR

At a formal boardroom ceremony in 1942, John David Eaton, the 33-year-old second son of Sir John Craig Eaton, assumed complete control of the Eaton empire. Although all four sons had been given full opportunity to prove their business ability ("We really watched those boys," recalls one of Sir John's executors), it was apparent from very early that John David stood out as the logical choice. Tim, the eldest, preferred his own pursuits of horses and hunting, historical lore and parade nights with his regiment, to the downtown turmoil of buying and selling. Edgar, whose childhood health had been delicate following almost fatal convulsions, was unequal to the rigours of a command post; after serving for a time in the Eaton insurance offices – where he is remembered for his sunny disposition and tall, blond attractiveness – he retired to private life on his suburban estate. Gilbert, the youngest, was still in the process of making his way up; eventually he became a department manager, and is today a Company director, as well as senior executive in the western division, with his headquarters in Winnipeg.

But it was John David who had done the slow, steady, thorough grind, as prescribed by father and grandfather, in absorbing the total atmosphere of the Company and its policies: first as salesclerk in Men's Furnishings, next as delivery-truck driver, then as department manager, store manager, director and, finally, after those twelve years of experience, to the head of the boardroom table.

He began his Eaton apprenticeship with a much

more diversified background than his forebears had achieved at his age – and this fact is directly traceable to an important decision by his mother after she had been left a widow. Determined that her children (for whom she was named sole guardian under her husband's will) would receive their education without favouritism or publicity due to their name or wealth, she had sent the three oldest boys to England, each to a different school; but after a few years this division of the family – half in Canada, half a full week's trip away – was too worrying, and besides *Ardwold* had become a lonely place. So Lady Eaton closed the big house on Toronto's Hill, and took up residence abroad, seeking a mild climate, on the doctor's advice, for the benefit of the younger children. Cannes was the first stop – and an important family event took place there with the adoption of a bright-eyed four-year-old, Evlyn Beatrice, as a companion for Florence Mary. The two girls became immediate friends with a closeness that has never wavered, and the whole process of adoption received its *cachet* of approval from all the Eatons as a result. Florence Mary, now Mrs Frank F. McEachren, adopted a daughter a few years after the birth of a son; Evlyn Beatrice, married to Russel T. Payton, is the mother of two girls and a "chosen" son.

Following the Cannes interlude, Lady Eaton moved her headquarters to Florence, Italy. Here in the beautiful *Villa Natalia*, built for Queen Elizabeth of Roumania (the romantic figure who had written folk tales and novels under the pen name of "Carmen Sylva" a half-century before), the main-line Eatons were to make their home for a number of years. At vacation periods the family circle was complete with the boys back from school; and even the staff personnel contributed to the reassuring normalcy of the atmosphere, for Lady Eaton had brought her *Ardwold* butler and his wife, and the chauffeur who taught all her children to drive and was for more than thirty years an essential member of the household.

Toronto did not enjoy losing sight of its most famous family during this period, and local gossips made the most of the stories brought back by travellers concerning the Eatons' Palladian palace and the salons crowded with faded luxury from the past (the owner-landlord was an antique dealer) and the gardens lavish with mimosa and camellias among the statuary.

Yet Lady Eaton did not live indolently in a Renaissance dream world. She engaged an expert in Italian history and art to tutor herself and her children and any visitors; once a week, rain or shine, one or two carloads moved off after breakfast to spend eight hours in educational sightseeing. Other days were given over to language lessons and music studies. Leaders in the current Florentine society called and found Milady from Canada an eager supporter of charities and concerts. Indeed, the European period of the Eatons was a busy one, and Mother was the organizer of all the activities, from winter-sports holidays in Switzerland to stern conferences in England concerning certain school reports. Today, looking back on those years, she says frankly, "I overdid it. I tried too hard to be both father and mother to my children. They would have done better without so much supervision."

From time to time she would make a whirlwind visit home – and it was characteristic of Lady Eaton that on one such occasion, a few weeks after her presentation at Court in London, she accepted a special engagement with the Eaton Girls' Club in Toronto to appear at their evening meeting in all her splendour of feathers, robe, and train, and to the delight of her audience performed the same deep curtsies she had dropped before the thrones of George V and Queen Mary.

It was well into the nineteen-thirties before all the members of the family were reunited in Canada – the girls through with their finishing school, the older sons already at their jobs in the Company. John David Eaton had come home after his final years of education at Corpus Christi College, Cambridge; he was fluent in French and German, proficient at many sports and, what was more to the point among the old-timers in the store, he already showed a marked resemblance to his father. True, he was a quieter type, less vivacious, more inclined to listen to a joke than tell one; nevertheless, the young man with the square-cut features of Sir John obviously enjoyed the comradeship of his fellow clerks among the Men's Shirts and Pyjamas, and was never averse to demonstrating his capacity to learn.

Shortly after he had officially turned the key at the opening of the College Street store, there was a casual announcement that John David would be leaving for a new post in the Winnipeg establishment. The newspaper reporters pursued President R. Y. with questions: "Did this mean some significant change?" "Not at all," was the answer. "He *works* – and this transfer is purely routine as part of our Company training program. It has no special significance."

This time, however, the President was off course. But he could hardly have foreseen that John David's western job would result in love and marriage and the introduction of an Icelandic strain to the solidly Irish Eaton line.

Signy Hilda Stefasson (sometimes Anglicized as "Stephenson") was just twenty years old in 1933 when she married John David Eaton, four years her senior. She was little and pretty, with the natural silvery blonde hair that distinguishes many Scandinavians. As the Winnipeg-born daughter of immigrants from the remote island of the north Atlantic, she had grown up equipped with both languages. The old tongue was used at home or among their many friends in the city's Icelandic community. Her father, a lithographer, was for a time partner-publisher of Winnipeg's first Icelandic-language newspaper. At high school, college, and later on entering the workaday world, she metamorphosed effortlessly into the all-Canadian girl, speaking English without a trace of accent, singing the popular songs of the day, fox-trotting at parties sufficiently select to gain her parents' permission to attend.

She possessed poise to a remarkable degree in one

so young. A few weeks before her marriage she was whisked off by Lady Eaton to England for presentation at Court, and went through the tiring formalities with calm precision. Next came the hurried return to Winnipeg, the final trousseau fittings, and the departure of the whole Stefasson family for Muskoka, where the wedding took place under a blue August sky in the gardens of *Kawandag*, the Eaton summer home. Thousands of newspaper readers devoured the carefully described details – the Union Jack and the flag of Iceland rippling together in the breeze . . . the aisle carpeted with sailcloth, the guest rows marked with knots and anchors, befitting a yachtsman's wedding . . . the bride picturesque in white chiffon over silver lamé, with filmy veil flowing from a winged Viking silver headdress . . . the flower borders a riot of colour . . . and the names of the guests, most of them relatives. It must have been, indeed, a perfect summer wedding, yet many of those present have their keenest enjoyment nowadays in reminiscing about the unreported occasion of the day before.

In Eaton annals this was to become known as "the Family Tree party." It started sedately enough – under the birches at Aunt Maggie Burden's place farther down the Lake Rosseau shore. Everybody was there, young and old, cousins and second cousins, in-laws present and future – all summoned to meet the little bride from the West, but with plenty of their own intimate chatter to exchange over the first round of cocktails.

"Lovely place, lovely people," remarked the bride-to-be to the tall black-haired man standing beside her. "But it's so hard to learn all your names and figure out just who belongs in which group."

"Well now," replied Hank Burden, cousin of John David, and one of Toronto's leading architects, "what you need is a family tree." In a few moments he had found a roll of shelf paper in the kitchen, torn off a length or two, tacked it to the porch wall, and, crayon in hand, started to draw and lecture at the same time. "Our subject today, ladies and gentlemen, is the *Ay*tons – who they are and how they got that way. Now it seems there was once a great lot of *Ay*tons living on a farm in An*th*rim. One little *Ay*ton went to market" (an outline of Timothy as a boy appeared on a branch). "Another little *Ay*ton stayed home" (R. Y.'s father took shape at an opposite point), and for the next hour there was no stopping him and no desire to. The party that might have had some stiffness and strain for a young bride-to-be romped to a hilarious finale. Among Mrs John David Eaton's personal souvenirs today is the rolled-up Family Tree drawing which, in spite of its zany cartoons and brash footnotes touching on many of the "*Ay*tons," performed such a happy service in initiating a newcomer into the clan.

The wedding was the last great event at *Kawandag*; a few years later the place was sold, and all attention turned on the new plan to build a big year-round headquarters at the Eaton farm near King, northwest of

Toronto and within easy driving distance from the city. From the time Sir John had purchased the first acreage with its woodland and beautiful sheet of water, the remodelled small farmhouse had served for weekends and picnics; modern barns, dairy, and greenhouses had been added; and now Lady Eaton became immersed in her project for a country house of size and atmosphere worthy enough to supersede *Ardwold.*

Eaton Hall achieved a miraculously mellow look right from the start. The warm brownish-grey stone from the valley of the Humber River a few miles away blends perfectly with the colours of beechwoods and pines and lawns and distant patches of ploughed earth. In style, too, the vast house suggests a settled serenity; the visitor, capturing glimpses of cone-topped towers and angled wings as the long winding drive brings him closer, might easily imagine himself in the chateau country of the Loire.

The interior plan makes full use of all the architectural features: a breakfast-room in one tower, an upstairs sitting-room in another; a main-floor great hall that stretches like an elongated hyphen between the two wings, one of which contains a music-room and panelled library, and the other the large formal dining-room in Louis XV period style, with kitchens, flower room, and so on, adjacent. Another dining-room with its services is a feature of the second floor; when Lady Eaton is in residence this smaller room with its *toile* wallpaper and French Provincial furniture provides the cheerful setting for lunch and dinner. Down the long corridor lined with paintings of Eaton and McCrea ancestors and their long-ago homes, she has her private apartment, consisting of bedroom, sunroom, and large sitting-room, complete with satinwood grand piano – one of four the house can boast. The ground floor, below the main rooms, contains two huge spaces designated as ballroom and sports room; these are used for large-scale entertaining – a Toronto ~ North York Hunt Club dance perhaps, or annual meetings of organizations, or a special Company party as when the elevator girls arrive in busloads for a festive dinner with their Eaton hosts. ("And I have never had nicer guests than our elevator girls," Lady Eaton remarks. "They made a delightful evening for us all.")

The property covers about 670 acres, of which half is actively worked; the gardens, woods, and Lake Jonda comprise the rest. A graduate agriculturist is in charge of all farm activities, and under the direction of John David Eaton the emphasis is on utility stock and production, rather than show-ring sensations. Nevertheless, *Eaton Hall* farm was awarded the coveted Master Breeder's Shield for its pure-bred Holstein herd, which in the spring of 1962 numbered ninety-five, with thirty-five being milked. Milk, eggs, and flowers are the farm's chief crops – the first sold through regular commercial channels, the eggs shipped to the Toronto store's restaurants and a few private buyers, and the potted plants and cut flowers ready in their hundreds and sometimes thousands for delivery to churches and family members' homes. In springtime two or three huge tractor-trailer vans are loaded with *Eaton Hall* flowering plants for the Toronto stores' fashion week.

The farm offers ample scope for the various hobbies and interests enjoyed by the Eatons of each generation. Lady Eaton, who makes the *Hall* her home for most of the year, is a passionate conservationist – as Toronto newspaper readers well know from her spirited letters to the editor on the subject. Through her steady efforts *Eaton Hall* farm has become a virtual laboratory of the outdoors, where a countless variety of trees, wild flowers, birds, and native animals can be studied by scientists and amateur enthusiasts. John David Eaton made his special contribution by expanding the recreational facilities of the property; some years ago he installed barbecues, games areas, diving-tower, wading-beach, and so on, on the far side of the lake and, through the store's Recreation Department, various clubs or King villagers could reserve a picnic date for a summer Saturday beside Lake Jonda, a half-mile away from the towers and terraces of the Norman French château. The President's two college-age sons have their fun at the farm by doing occasional "roadwork" in their racing cars along the private drives.

Personal memories of *Eaton Hall* and its magnificence, outside and in, are probably cherished by many people around the world. During the first years of the Second World War seven children and two mothers from the United Kingdom were duration guests; Lady Eaton had the complete responsibility for their support in Canada. Toward the end of that period the house was turned over to the Royal Canadian Navy as a convalescent home.

The first big peacetime occasion had its poignant wartime atmosphere, too, for in the autumn of 1946 *Eaton Hall* was the setting for the welcome-home party given by John David Eaton and his Directors to all Ontario veterans, men and women, and the next-of-kin of those who had laid down their lives. There were a few brief speeches to the multitude assembled on the lawn: the President expressed his pride in the record of the 5,615 Eatonians from all parts of Canada who had served their country, and a spokesman for the guests conveyed the thanks of Eaton men for the Company's generosity in the matter of "duration pay" (the same system as obtained under Sir John in the First World War). In the following weeks Mr and Mrs Eaton led a delegation to similar Eaton veteran reunions in other provinces. Every ex-service person attending received a gold signet ring designed with a commemorative device.

This year, 1963, marks the twenty-first anniversary of the presidency of John David Eaton. He is supreme ruler of a realm that has no near counterpart. It is a family business, totally Canadian, and in its major activities totally "private," with no obligation to issue annual statements or balance sheets.

True, there are a few relatively small segments within the composite structure which, because of the nature of their operations, publish regular financial reports. The T. Eaton Life Assurance Company is a chartered life insurance organization, conducting its business in the same way as outside competitors in the field, with its own funds, investments and Board of Directors (some of them Eaton men, others non-Eaton); it is fully qualified to accept insurance commitments from any source. However, as there is no active soliciting among the general public, about 95 per cent of Eaton Life's service is with Eaton employees, past and present. The annual statement dated March 1963 showed total business in force of over $218,000,000, an increase of 12.8 per cent over the previous year. Another grouping publishing regular balance sheets is The T. Eaton Realty Co., Limited, set up some thirty years ago as a lease-holding authority for certain Company properties; there are today about $15,000,000 of its gilt-edged bonds in the hands of the investing public.

But outside of these few separate sections, the Company remains the same closely guarded private enterprise as it was in the founder's time. The dollar value of Eaton's of Canada is anybody's guess – and this has an excellent chance of being wrong. Such matters as total capital, gross earnings, operating costs, net profits and the like can only be mused over, like any heady subject suitable for day-dreaming, such as life on Mars, or the mileage of gold-paved streets in paradise.

The President is generally conceded to be Canada's richest man, and this opinion became a fairly substantial fact in the year 1948 when he made his own personal contribution of $50,000,000 to the launching of the Eaton employees' contributory pension fund – a gift which enabled payment of immediate benefits to men and women approaching retirement age. It is doubtful if any other Canadian citizen could approach that scale of wealth-sharing.

John David Eaton is fifty-four years old, and most of his downtown associates have dropped the adjective from the once-familiar phrase, "young Mr Eaton." In appearance he has weathered, become rather thick-set in spite of watching his weight, but the mind that directs Eaton's of Canada is a cutting edge, honed brighter and sharper with the postwar years and their problems, opportunities, and achievements.

The business which he inherited – even then a vast complex of activities – has zoomed ahead with the speed of the new jet age. The emphasis today is almost entirely on merchandising and customers' services. With the industrial growth of the country and the constantly expanding sources of supply, the Eaton factories, so important half a century ago, have gradually been closed down, leaving just three or four in Ontario to fill very specific needs. Nevertheless, Eaton's own brand-name lines, manufactured to very precise Company specifications, continue to go on from strength to strength, and range all the way from Viking television sets to Gleneaton nylon hosiery and each day's fresh batch of Cottage Sweets candies. The Company's oldest brand name, of course, is Timothy's proud creation, "Eatonia," which may appear at any counter or on any type of merchandise, so long as the article meets the carefully maintained standard of "outstanding value at a popular price."

A significant extension of the Eaton empire took place in 1948 with the purchase of the Spencer chain of department stores in British Columbia. At the time of the official change-of-command, Mr Chris Spencer, President of that 75-year-old family firm, stated smilingly, "The T. Eaton Company, which for many years wanted to extend its business to Vancouver – and only put it off because we were very great friends – recently decided it couldn't wait any longer." He reported that offers from other organizations and other countries had also been received, "but I think you will consider the present course the natural one and best for all concerned." He praised the Spencer staff of 8,500 men and women, and promised their loyal co-operation with the new owners.

Within a matter of a few hours the first Eaton directives were issued, and they were reassuringly typical: (1) tobacco counters in the British Columbia stores were to be removed immediately; (2) blinds must be drawn across store windows on Sundays.

By the early nineteen-fifties Eaton's had expanded their on-the-spot merchandising operations to all ten provinces, and the new name, "Eaton's of Canada," was proudly presented to the public from coast to coast.

Although Eaton outlets seldom stand still long enough to be accurately counted, it may be considered safe to describe the picture as it was in October 1962. There were then seventy-two Eaton stores, embracing nineteen main stores and forty-five branch stores, plus a few other categories. These seventy-two selling establishments pinpointed the Eaton map all the way from Gander, Newfoundland, to Victoria, British Columbia.

At that same autumn census-taking, there were three Catalogue houses (the up-to-date version of Mail Order headquarters), forty-eight "heavy goods" display centres for such Catalogue items as washing-machines and refrigerators, and 345 Catalogue sales (order) offices, including one in Whitehorse, Yukon Territory.

The Catalogue itself had reached a total annual circulation of over 17,000,000 copies; these broke down into several editions – one for Spring-Summer, another for Fall-Winter (each over four hundred pages thick, and splashed with full-colour illustrations), plus smaller mid-season or special pre-Christmas issues. Eaton's Catalogues still list such sturdy down-to-earth essentials as "chamber pots, medium size," and "box stoves, wood-burning," but in the thousands of modern articles offered the appeal is definitely urban rather than rural. In fact, there is a new boom on, in cities and Suburbia, for Catalogue shopping.

A couple of big shiny Eaton Automotive Centres – one in Toronto, the other in Vancouver – marked a new phase in servicing and selling to the motoring public.

And, also in the fall of '62, the average employee payroll for the total Eaton enterprise across Canada – exclusive of "occasional" help before Christmas and other crescendo seasons – stood at over 40,000. Outside of Canada there were ten buying-offices or agencies, spanning half the world as the sun travels, between Frankfurt in Germany and the swarming marts of the Orient.

But, as always there is more Eaton history just around the next corner. Soon the Yorkdale Shopping Centre, just northwest of Toronto at highway junction points, will open; on its eighty-acre site (acquired by Eaton's some years ago) Canada's largest modern retail-plaza development will present the competitive blandishments of both Eaton's and Simpson's, plus ninety other shops. The Eaton emporium there will have 362,000 square feet of floor space, with an added 30 per cent capacity for expansion. Doubtless before Yorkdale is ready for the public, contractors will be at work on another shopping-centre project, recently announced, for Pointe Claire, the populous suburban area near Montreal.

The President keeps all these details at his fingertips. For quick on-the-spot inspection of work in progress, he and top executives find it handy to use his Lockheed Jetstar – a four-engine pure jet, bought two years ago at a cost of $1,000,000 stripped – which stands by, ready at any hour of day or night to speed them on their business travels. Three other planes of various types, for various duties, complete the Eaton air fleet in 1963.

Family members who do not have the benefit of boardroom briefing have learned to brace themselves for Company surprises almost every time they read a newspaper. In 1961 there were bold headlines over the announcement that Eaton's would open "bargain centres" as a direct answer to the stiff competition from discount houses; the first would be part of the new service centre (a building almost one mile in circumference, located in the Toronto suburbs). Far away in Stockholm, the President's mother, winding up a European holiday with a visit to the Canadian Embassy, casually picked up that edition of her hometown paper and was stunned by what she read. Back in *Eaton Hall* twenty-four hours later, she was on the telephone to her son. "What's all this about bargain centres? Are we going to start a place like Honest Ned's?" A few soothing chuckles at the other end of the line, and then the firm statement, "You should know, Mother, that anything they can do, we can do better."

Certainly he should know, too, for there is no form or phase of modern merchandising that has escaped his appraising eye. He has studied the methods of United States and United Kingdom retailing, and a few years ago made a special tour of the state-operated department stores in Russia. And, in reverse order, there is seldom a week without its quota of managing-director visitors to his Toronto office. Macy's of New York sends top men regularly to view the Santa Claus Parade down University Avenue. In 1955 there was a sizable delegation of executive observers from that store and Bamberger's of New Jersey; after watching the procession, in which eleven hundred people took part, they expressed amazement at Eaton's wardrobe resources and the quality and freshness of the costumes.

Outside of the Company Mr Eaton restricts his business involvements, although he manages to allow some time for the Toronto newspaper, *The Telegram,* in which he shares a financial interest with his friend, the publisher. The Ontario Crippled Children's Centre, of which he is Chairman, gets more of his spare hours than any other enterprise, and the opening of the cheerful, perfectly equipped building for treatment and training of handicapped boys and girls brought in from any point in the province, was an occasion for great rejoicing by him and his committee.

Like his Eaton forefathers he delights in the new and the better, and building for improved service of a proved need. As a trustee of the Timothy Eaton Memorial Church he had been aware of the growth of the congregation (now four thousand) and the pressure on facilities. So, in 1962, the church passed a notable landmark with the opening of a new wing, containing an auditorium to seat five hundred, banquet facilities, meeting-rooms, offices for minister and staff. Until the ceremony of dedication, the name of the friend who had donated the full cost of the handsome stone addition – approximately $700,000 – had been kept secret. When the draperies were pulled back from the datestone and the carved inscription read to the vast crowd of onlookers, among them Lady Eaton, there were two glad surprises to draw rounds of applause and standing ovations: Mr and Mrs John David Eaton were the donors of the building "in honor of Lady Eaton," and this section of the great church would bear the name of The Flora McCrea Eaton Building.

Most of the Company benefactions pass under the President's review, and they are an almost daily occurrence. Hospitals, scholarships, the Drama Festival, university building campaigns, dozens of Community Chests across the country – these are mere samples from a list that runs over many pages in current Company files. A few years ago McGill University marked a notable event with the opening of the Eaton Electronics Research Laboratory, a gift of the President and Company. Perhaps today there are fewer folksy charities, in contrast with the old times when Flora McCrea Eaton "oiled the roads" of her native village of Omemee every summer with her personal cheque; but the times themselves have changed, and gifts to organized groups with fixed goals ensure "the greatest good for the greatest number" – in the favourite words of Grandfather Timothy.

And the founder's influence is strong even yet. In the President's office there is a leather-bound journal in T. Eaton's handwriting, recording thoughts, mottoes, and business principles as they inspired the bearded man at his rolltop desk far back in the 'eighties. In the Advertising Departments of the Company the old rules concerning honesty and "no false enthusiasm" are still stressed in the up-to-date handbook which is the copywriter's constant companion; under "Taboo Words and

Phrases" are listed such adjectives as "amazing," "best," "phenomenal," which must never be used as *descriptive of merchandise*; other words such as "unshrinkable" and "fast colours" are permissible only "if sanction is first obtained from the Research Bureau."

Like his forefathers, John David Eaton loves his home and loves being there. With a few friends he relaxes into a genial host, pouring the drinks, offering the box of cigarettes (and generally apologizing for their possible staleness . . . nobody in the house smokes), and teasing his wife about her latest art treasures. The big handsome rooms are quietly modern, in keeping with the highly Continental style of the exterior of the house, with its planes and overhangs and smooth, unbroken expanses of white brick and glass. The background throughout hall, drawing-room, and library is unpatterned and neutral, chiefly in soft beige or pale champagne tones; against this the pictures attain their full visibility. The names are mostly of the great French twentieth-century period – Utrillo, Bracque, Picasso, Renoir, Dufy – and the pieces are impressively representative of the individual artist's full flowering. One of Henry Moore's vigorous linear sculptures surmounts a cabinet. A few fine antiques – eighteenth-century Italian painted chairs, for example – add interesting variety to the groups of curved modern settees and low tables. Near the fireplace rests a graceful pottery jar, about three feet tall; it is encrusted with tiny glistening shells and shows mysterious scarring and colour gradations here and there. The jar was a triumphant find of Mrs Eaton in a grocery store in the island of Patmos, during a cruise with her husband through the Greek archipelago. It had been just previously dredged up from the harbour where, according to reports of Toronto museum experts after careful examination, it must have lain among the rocks and sand for nineteen centuries.

The house is a thoroughly comfortable, lived-in place, but for its restrained décor, priceless art objects, openness of space and originality of plan, it has been voted unique by hundreds, perhaps thousands, of Toronto people. They have visited 120 Dunvegan Road (no fancy name – just a street number) during the many organized fund-raising teas and musicales for which the Eatons have lent their house. Only recently has this type of request subsided, and Mr J. D., for one, is happy to have his house back again. "It's nice to come to my own front door and not have to pay to get in," he tells his wife.

There is always plenty of busy family life going on. The two younger boys, Thor Edgar and George Ross Eaton, enjoy the big recreation room downstairs for their soirées; here they have access to hi-fi, piano, dance floor, long snack bar with complete service for ice-cold pop, sandwiches, hot dogs – everything the young heart desires. The two older sons are away, in homes of their own. Fredrik Stefan, married to Katherine Martin of Hamilton and in April 1963 presented with a son, is a keen young executive at Eaton's in Victoria on the

West Coast; he probably has little time nowadays for the hobbies he pursued while a student at the University of New Brunswick in Fredericton, where he conducted a popular television program, worked on the campus paper, and gave impromptu evenings of modern music in his quarters.

John Craig Eaton II is the eldest son and for the past seven or eight years has been gathering experience in various Company posts, in Toronto or beyond. When he and his wife, the former Kitty Farr, are based in their home town, they gladly make use of the "sitter" service which is almost always available at his parents' big house. The first grandchild, another John David, rates as just about the most popular guest at 120 Dunvegan Road. On one occasion the grandfather, after a happy Sunday afternoon session with his namesake, handed the baby over to the young couple with the comment, "I can hardly bear to let this boy go. You people have just got to have another baby for yourselves!" Obligingly they did – with the birth of Signy Catherine. In 1963 a second son, Henry Craig, joined the group.

Mrs John David Eaton divides her time between the supervision of the town house, the year-round weekend house in the Caledon Hills, and the spacious summer home on a Georgian Bay island – plus a busy calendar of outside duties. In addition to the numerous Company occasions and trips with her husband, she is active in women's associations at the Eaton Memorial Church, and twice a week takes her place as the first woman member of the Board of Governors of York University. She is still, however, the composed, unhurried, agreeable Signy of her bridal days; her slim figure, tailored clothes, smooth complexion, and fair hair that has slightly darkened but never greyed, make her grandmother status hard to believe.

The John David Eatons live their rich life quietly. The President puts his own special value on anonymity. Although there are big haughty cars in his garage, he likes to drive his Volks downtown each morning. Admittedly, the 104-foot yacht, a ketch-rigged motor-sailer, equipped with radar screen and every modern navigational device, is a luxury of the exotic kind; it was built to his order in Vancouver shipyards in 1959, christened *Hildur* (the Icelandic form of his wife's second name), and has logged many thousands of miles through the Caribbean, across the Atlantic, into the Mediterranean and elsewhere. But once aboard with his captain and crew and his wife and boys, John David Eaton achieves the peace and relaxation difficult to come by in any other environment. If it's an all-male fishing expedition off the Florida Keys or at the top of Georgian Bay, he and his guests generally agree to skip such nuisances as shaving, shoes, shirts, ties. "I've seen those men come ashore looking like hoboes," declares one of the wives.

The President and his mother have some brisk arguments from time to time about their separate hobbies or indulgences. If he makes a comment about the big house she keeps in town but seldom stays in, she reminds him about the *Hildur*, idling for months at a time in a Florida berth. (Lady Eaton has simply never enjoyed luxury yachts or yachting at any stage in her long career.)

But the mother-son relationship is a solid one, with deepest respect on both sides. John David Eaton is supreme ruler of his empire, and the final counsel on all business affairs, whether concerned with family or Company; his mother has complete confidence in his wisdom and is proud to accept his decisions. Lady Eaton is the head of the family, the active clan memory that encompasses the history, triumphs, and crises affecting all the Eatons in their Canadian progress; the strong link between then and now. For sixty-two years she has watched Eaton's four Presidents at work, been privy to their secret dreams of still greater accomplishment, and witnessed achievements that far surpassed even the most optimistic hopes.

There is just one important matter still outstanding, awaiting the proper moment. Careful approaches in Ireland by Eaton diplomats have not yet won a certain landlord's permission to erect a memorial plaque at the old Clogher farm. There is a noisy, happy Eaton recreation park in Ballymena (a post-war gift of today's President), but the birthplace of the man who founded the family and its fortune is still unmarked. One of these days, though – perhaps for the hundredth anniversary of the Company – the Eatons will find a way. They always have.

FAMILY TREE OF EATON PRESIDENTS

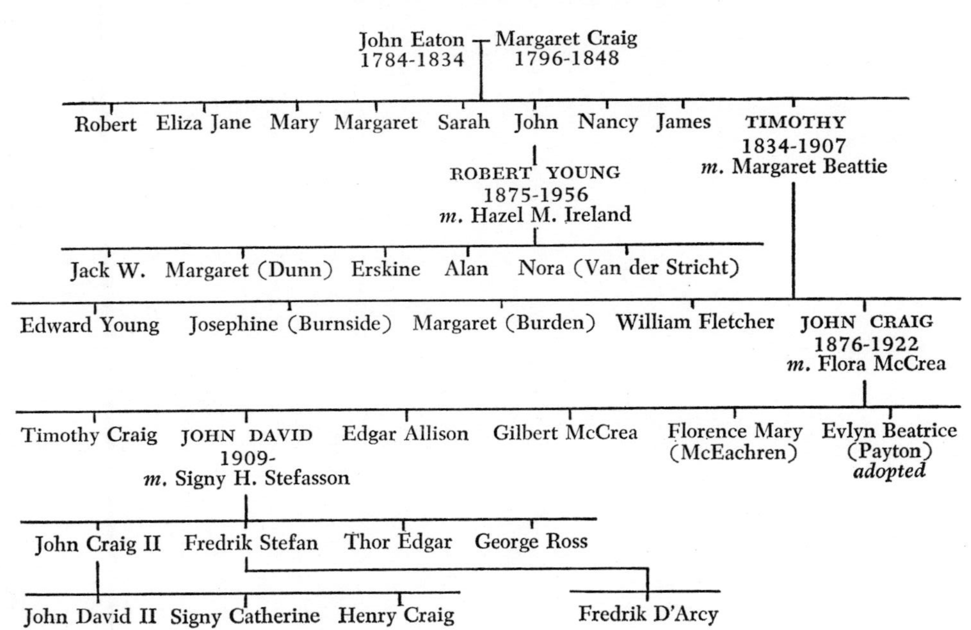

ACKNOWLEDGEMENTS

This story of the Eatons, from the Clogher Farm of 1834 to the Canada of the nineteen-sixties, has been several years in preparation, and is herewith presented for the first time in its complete form. At the request of *Chatelaine*, a series of three excerpts, having chiefly to do with the various personalities among the Eaton generations, was prepared for publication in the 1962 June, July, and August issues of that magazine. Now the original full manuscript, updated to midsummer of 1963, is seeing the light of day and, in the ampler vehicle of an individual book, perhaps better able to convey the importance of Company developments as they occurred during the various presidential regimes, and which, by their kind and scope, serve to demonstrate the character and methods of each chief executive in turn. This work, however, does not purport to be a complete history of Eaton's of Canada; indeed, such a project would – and no doubt some day will – challenge the acuity of an expert historian-*cum*-economist, and result in several well-filled volumes.

Among the valuable sources of information for the present story have been: *Timothy Eaton*, by George G. Nasmith (McClelland and Stewart Limited, 1923); *Golden Jubilee: 1869-1919*, prepared and printed by The T. Eaton Co., Limited, 1919; and *Memory's Wall*, Lady Eaton's autobiography (Clarke, Irwin & Co., Ltd., 1956).

Eaton's Archives office, organized some years ago for the collection and preservation of records and souvenirs bearing on Company and family history, has provided unfailingly alert, generous help throughout the author's months of research. All illustrations have been supplied by courtesy of that department.

Interviews with various descendants of the Clogher Farm Eatons have yielded a rich harvest of memories and anecdotes concerning the several generations of this large family connection.

For all such sources of assistance, the author wishes to express warmest thanks.

INDEX